The Law & Burning Problems

The daring publisher, Universal Law Publishing Company, among the foremost in the law publishing field and progressive in venturing to bring out rare legal literature of avant garde *character has rightly enriched the* corpus juris *of India*

Justice V R Krishna Iyer
Random Reflections, page 14

The Law & Burning Problems

V.K.S. Chaudhary
Senior Advocate
Ex. Advocate General, U.P.

Universal
Law Publishing Co. Pvt. Ltd.
NEW DELHI - INDIA

2013 Edition

ISBN: 978-93-5035-331-8

Published by
UNIVERSAL LAW PUBLISHING CO. PVT. LTD.
C-FF-1A, Dilkhush Industrial Estate,
(Near Azadpur Metro Station) G.T. Karnal Road,
Delhi-110 033
Tel.: 011-47082254, 27438103, 27215334
Fax : 011-27458529
E-mail *(For sales inquiries)* : unilaw@vsnl.com
(For editorial inquiries) : edit@unilawbooks.com
Website : www.unilawbooks.com
Join us on Facebook
www.facebook.com/unilawbooks

Recommended citation: VKS Chaudhary, *The Law & Burning Problems* (New Delhi: Universal Law Publishing Co. Pvt. Ltd., 2013).

Computer Typeset at Aesthetic and *Printed* at Glorious Printers, New Delhi.

In the Memory of my parents

Th. Keshav Chandra Singh Chaudhary,

Advocate, Banda (U.P.)

and

Smt. Rajdulari Devi

Acknowledgement

I have to acknowledge my debt to the authors for quotations, which have been borrowed and reproduced in the articles. I also thank my clerk Sri Shivsagar for typing the manuscript on the computer and to Sri Rajeshwar Tripathi LL.M. for revising the computerized version for any mistakes and to Sri Kunal Ravi Singh LL.M., advocate, High Court for re-checking the references therein. The views expressed in this book are mine.

April 2013 **VKS CHAUDHARY**

(Senior Advocate and Ex-Advocate-General, U.P.)
37, Tashkend Marg, Allahabad-211001
Telephones (0532) 2622950, 2624891

Introduction

1. Nearly 63 years have passed since the Constitution of India came into operation. Yet we are beset with some burning problems churning the minds of the nation. Object of a Constitution is to weld the nation as an integrity. What has happened in this long period to create problems instead of remedying them? The lawyers and the court must also share the blame. How have the problems arisen, which are embroiling the nation today?

2. Our Constitution tried to abolish caste. Differences will arise if we stress upon them. Their appeasement is counter-productive. On the other hand, we should know what is 'caste' and how it arose. There is a colossal misunderstanding about its meaning and origin. The foreign writers have misrepresented it. In the freedom struggle we forgot caste. Our minds were flushed with the dream of independence. The first chapter is concerned with the caste reservation. All reservation contravene the basic structure of the Constitution, that of equality. The reverse discrimination by law or amendment of the Constitution is now *ultra vires* the amending powers of the Parliament.

3. The second basic problem is misunderstanding about 'secularism'. How this word came into vogue? How has the Supreme Court of United States of America (USA) confronted with the same problem and tackled it? It is regrettable that we have not learnt the lesson from judicial history of various nations.

4. The next problem has been created regarding the marriage law by the *Khap* agitation. This problem is dealt with in this chapter.

5. 'The story re-told' is partly to tell the readers what I knew about the incident of demolition of the structure at Sri Ram Janmabhoomi in Ayodhya. It has been necessitated as the incident has been glossed over by purposive falsehoods. I was Advocate-General of Uttar Pradesh at that time and various incidents took place in my knowledge.

6. 'Cry Ayodhya Cry' relates to gross abdication of its functions by the Allahabad High Court (Lucknow Bench). Seervai in his famous book on Constitution of India has some thing to say about a similar judgment of the Supreme Court. He has written about such abandonment of its role that 'one has to hang his head in shame about such lapses of the court'. And why sermonize about the abandonment of one's role.

7. The Kashmir problem seemed to be unsolvable by the Congress leaders. The next chapter 'The Kashmir Imbroglio' deals with it. It was written at the time when ***Keshvananda Bharti's* case, (1972) 4 SCC 275** see page 1007: AIR 1973 SC 1461, (*see* the summary at the end) was not well-settled as some doubts have been raised at the judgment of the Single Judge (H R Khanna J) which become the final judgment of the Bench. Now it is well-settled that the Constitution cannot be amended to change the basic features of the Constitution. Another section has therefore been added to it. The problem is now with the Courts to adjudicate on the amending power under article 370 (3).

8. Then follow three articles on Education and the Law. The first deals with aberrations in law: the 'flim-flam' of the Union Government. Incidentally, I have dealt with the freedom struggle and what Constituent Assembly meant.

9. The next two articles under the heading, 'Education and the Law' previously comprised one article. The first part was the 'Supreme Court and Minority Institutions'. It is a vexed question, especially in the background of 'terrorism' the world over. I have separated the last article, 'the Monkey Trial' as it contained a lesson. India cannot afford to forget. Incidentally, these articles refer to decisions of the Supreme Court of USA as they dealt with education in the light of 'secularism', the basic feature of our Constitution meaning 'a divorce between religion and the State'.

10. I never wanted to pen down this last chapter, 'Lest We Forget', at the end of my career as a lawyer. But my friends said, "If you don't write about them, nobody else can. How will the future Judges running the High Courts and the Supreme Court know the qualities required and ideal expected of them or the qualities any Judge should emulate". Very few Judges know about the travails of the British Rule or framing of the Constitution, which every citizen should know.

11. A grave duty is cast on the Supreme Court of India and the lawyers to give effect to the Constitution. This requires an understanding of the problems now confronting the country. Some of them have been created by the Courts themselves as they never addressed the basic question, 'what the provision meant to the Constituent Assembly.' Not what politicians think it means or suits them? If we ask wrong questions we are likely to get wrong answers. It is with fond hope that a rethinking will start now to fulfil the great task expected of the judiciary to weld the nation.

VKS CHAUDHARY

(Senior Advocate and Ex-Advocate-General, U.P.)
37, Tashkend Marg, Allahabad-211001
Telephones (0532) 2622950, 2624891

CONTENTS

TABLE OF CASES

I

K

L

M

P

R

S

T

U

V

W

CHAPTER 1

Reservation Now of Any Kind is Unconstitutional

I. Introductory

1. The question, whether reservation of any kind or its continuance in any part now is constitutional is agitating the country. It has stirred the feelings of the nation and torn the country into antagonistic groups. The inquiry into the whole problem can be divided into three parts. *Firstly,* whether reservation is at all warranted or can be enacted under article 15(4) of the Constitution. *Secondly* reservation under article 16(4) and *Thirdly* the reservation in the election of legislature and the various bodies of the local self-government and other units of society.

2. All exercise in interpretation is to find out the intention of the enacting body. Constitution has to be interpreted by finding out why the provision was inserted in the Constitution and what it meant to the Constituent Assembly and not what it means today to the political parties.

II. Right to 'Equality' Before the 'Law'

3. No society (much less a State) can exist long without basic attribute of equality among its individual members or constituents. The Supreme Court has recognized this by calling *'equality before the law and equal protection of the laws'* as a basic feature and tenet of the Constitution. It is thus enshrined in article 14 and subsequent articles of the chapter on Fundamental Rights. It is the golden thread, which binds a nation.

4. The quest for equality has gone on throughout the ages the world over. The concept however continues to elude mankind. It is mainly so, as we have hankered after it at the wrong places. According to *Smritikars* in ancient law, *'samata'* (equality) arises out of inner consciousness that 'God or the Divine resides in every one'. This means that it does not lie in *'ekrupta'* (identity of form) but in *'ekatmata'* (oneness of the soul) or *'samrasta'* (equanimity). The two concepts of equality are poles apart; *'ekrupta'* leads to struggle and disruption, while *'samrasta'* leads to unity and strength. So-called 'social structuring' can only be based on *'samrasta'*. Any other method will either lead to fissiparous tendencies in the society or will violate the mandate of equality. (Contrast it with Muslims and Christians: "There will be equality if everybody adopted the Muslim or the Christian faith".

5. In my childhood days, those now induced to class themselves among the 'backward' or 'lower' castes craved to be identified with those they termed as 'higher castes' or superiors and began to claim from them. They took on a mass scale the caste appellations of so-called 'higher castes'. 'Ahirs' and 'Yadavs' began calling themselves *'yadu-vanshi thakurs'*, Kurmis *'kurma kshatriya'*, and 'Lodhs' began to call themselves *'lodh rajputs'* and were welcomed as such. They, in conformity with what might have been their initial status, tried to emulate the qualities associated with the higher values and shun departures from the path of rectitude. Thus, came *'bhagats'* among them, teaching of a few of them are still remembered with pride in the Hindu society. They advocated a chaste life, a life of devotion and honour, not to a caste, but to the society irrespective of caste, the vision of sublime existence, human values and oneness of the society. This is the way of *'samrasta'*, the ultimate blending in one whole. They never claimed to be leaders of their caste, but spoke of and to the Hindu society, nay the whole humanity.

6. Unfortunately, the way of equanimity has been abandoned by populist political sloganeering, which creates a personal stake or vested interest in caste. Instead of unity, it breeds acrimony, resulting in disunity and ever-increasing claims for higher reservation, nay proportional representation to their 'supposed' number ('supposed' because there is no recent census on the basis of caste). The so-called castes that repudiated their earlier supposed status and had joined the other castes now feel sorry for it and have tried to fall back upon professional archaic names.

7. This search for equality the world over has taken a zig-zag course. In USA, it began in 1896 with the decision. In ***Plessy* v. *Ferguson*, 41 Law Ed 256**, when the Louisiana statute requiring segregation was held not to violate the equality clause. 'Separate but equal' formula was blessed by the courts. It said,

> "The object was undoubtedly to enforce absolute equality before the law, but in the nature of things it could not have been intended to abolish the distinction based on colour or to enforce social as distinct from political equality or co-mingling of two races upon terms unsatisfactory to either".

It was a long journey to 1994, when the Supreme Court of USA.

In ***Brown* v. *Board of Education of Topeka*, 99 Law Ed 1083** enunciated what was exactly the opposite. Said the Court, ***"Allegedly equal but separate educational facilities are inherently unequal".*** This started a series of de-segregation school cases.

8. Both the articles 15 and 16 (as well as that follow) are different facets of 'equality' embodied in article 14 of the Constitution. They state the universal rule embodied in particular cases and also enumerate certain exceptions necessitated by change over from the foreign rule and an agglomeration of what were called Indian States to a democratic entity and for historical and other reasons. Thus sub-articles 15(1), 15(2) and 16(1), 16(2) state the general rule, while those that follow are exceptions, required to produce an egalitarian social order. It must, therefore, be borne in mind that the first two sub-articles lay down the general rule, while the rest are exceptions. The object is to lift certain classes by removing the deficiency noted therein to enable them to flow with the national stream of life.

III. Questions 1 and 2

9. Thus, the very first thing to notice is that these exceptions must be temporary or short-lived. They were considered essential for removal of deficiency or disparities noted therein in what may be termed as 'classes' of the society. But when their deficiency is removed, they rank with the rest of citizens and stand with them partaking on equal footing in the life of a nation. The aim is not to create more or another class of citizens but to eliminate what may be called 'disabilities' of that 'class'. There can be no secondary class of citizens in a nation. The whole purpose is to get rid of or annihilate, in the political field, any subordinate class, whatever might be the cause and to create one harmonious cadre of citizens.

10. A comparison of the provisions of articles 15 and 16 *(as they stood when the Constitution came into force)* are revealing. They are different and distinct.

- **(i)** They deal with different types of backward classes. Article 15(4) (*added by the Constitution First Amendment*) talks of socially and educationally backward class of citizens and of the Scheduled Castes and Scheduled Tribes. It is noteworthy that backward classes are separately classed from Scheduled Castes and Scheduled Tribes. Article 16 speaks of a different class of citizens, which in the opinion of the State, is not adequately represented in its services. Again the Constitutional amendments draw a distinction between backward classes and the Scheduled Castes and Scheduled Tribes.
- **(ii)** Clearly they have different objects in view. Article 15(4) speaks of special provisions by law for advancement of socially and educationally backward classes *i.e.* for their social and educational

uplift. The other provision provides for reservation in appointments or posts under the State.

(iii) The remedies suggested are also different. Adequate representation of any class in the services and posts under the State can be measured, while social and educational backwardness cannot be so measured. The later are elusive factors and differ from place and climate and individuals and other imponderables. At any rate, there can be no objective test for them common to a class (except possibly the Scheduled Castes and Scheduled Tribes, which are separately mentioned and stand apart).

11. The provision of 'equality before the law and equal protection of the laws' for every person (article 14) is a basic feature of the Constitution. Articles 15 and 16 are only different facets of it. They specifically prohibit discrimination against any citizen on stated grounds, including race, caste or religion (and descent in article 16). In case of discrimination on other grounds one has to fall back on the general prohibition contained in article 14. The gamut of articles under the heading *'Right to Equality'* when read together demonstrate that equality is the rule and special provisions or reservation for any section or class of people, which obviously contradicts the rule, are exceptions.

12. That these exceptions are meant to be transient, for the time being only, and cannot be a basic feature of the Constitution, follows from their very object, the Constituent Assembly debates, and the spirit behind article 334. Special provisions can exist for the purpose of advancement of socially and educationally backward class of citizens, so that persons constituting it may join the main stream of the nation, *vide* article 15(4). In article 16(4), reservation exists for another backward class, one which is not adequately represented in the services of the State, till they acquire such a place therein [*See* article 16(4)]. The avowed purpose in the two cases is different. But when the object is achieved, there will no longer be any need for special provision or reservation. Expressing the same in dialectics, the object of special provision or reservation is to end them and give effect to the basic tenet of equality.

13. In case 'class' is taken to mean caste, the transient nature of the provision regarding reservation is lost, as caste inherited from father to son, goes on. It can end only by repealing the enumeration of caste in defining a class. We know how caste reservation has been abused.

14. The provisions of articles 15(4) and 16(4), being meant for different classes, circumstances and being distinct, the remedies suggested are also at variance with each other. They cannot obviously be grouped together, yet (in our humble opinion) a mistake was committed in taking them together in the case of:

***Indra Sawhney* v. *Union of India*, AIR 1993 SC 477: 1992 Supp SCC 217: 1902 AIR SCW 3682** *(often alluded to as the Mandal Commission* case). It is strange that in that lengthy judgment of majority judges, this distinction was not emphasized with the result that all later judgments went awry. Supreme Court elevated what was merely an exception to the pedestal of a fundamental right; what was a temporary measure to be thus a permanent feature of the Constitution. Sri Seervai, one of the foremost constitutional experts in his famous treatise on *Indian Constitutional Law* (Vol. III page 2928) has the following comment to offer—

> "With rare exceptions the standard of Supreme Court has continued to fall steeply in matters involving questions of Constitutional Law, (and) the judgments of five majority judges on article 16(4) (of the Constitution) have reached the rock bottom.... (N)ever have 6 Supreme Court Judges served the Bench, the Bar and the general public so ill as the majority (in *Mandal Commission* case) have served them".

15. The Supreme Court of USA has remarked, "Our Constitution is colour blind". Could our Courts not say (paraphrasing the words and purport of the minority judgment of Sri R.M. Sahai J. in that case, "Our Constitution is caste blind". The observations in that case relating to article 15(4) are *'per in curium'* and do not constitute a precedent.

16. As noted earlier the word 'reservation' has not been used in article 15(4) in the remedy suggested, as in article 16(4). When a statute uses two different sets of words or phraseology at two proximate places, they obviously mean two different remedies and apply to two different situations. The use of word reservation in article 16(4), where there can be an objective test, cannot be applied to a case of article 15(4) under the guise of interpreting the word 'special provisions' as contemplated by article 15(4). This interpretation as dealt later is not warranted by article 368; article 15(4) was introduced by the first Constitutional Amendment under article 368 of the Constitution.

17. Regard being had to articles 15(1), 15(2) and 16(1) and 16(2) and reading articles 15(4) and 16(4) in their light it is apparent that sub-articles (1) and (2) lay down the general rule and sub-article (4) is an exception. An exception from its very nature cannot take the place of a general rule. Article 15(4) cannot be elevated to the pedestal of a fundamental right as was sought to be done in ***Indra Sawhney's*** **case**. Thus, the various statutes, rules or notifications purporting to be made under article 15(4) are unconstitutional.

18. Provisions of article 16(4) (as it originally stood) and reservations relating to special provisions were meant for Scheduled Castes and Scheduled Tribes. To understand the reason, we must first investigate who are Scheduled Castes and Scheduled Tribes.

19. Scheduled Castes and Scheduled Tribes stand apart for historical reasons. It was so noted by the Constituent Assembly.

- **(a)** They did not exist in the ancient Hindu Society. There is no Hindu scripture or text sanctioning untouchability. These are a result of foreign invasion and rule. Recent researches throw a great deal of light on their genesis.
- **(b)** Slavery (where men, women and children were property and could be sold and purchased) was unknown to ancient India. *'Kautaliya Arthshastra'* (the ancient political treatise) says, "no Indian can

be a slave". But slavery was prevalent from ancient times in Arabia, Africa and Europe. When Muslim invaders came, they brought with them 'slavery' also as practiced in those parts. The first victims to be made slaves were 'war-prisoners'. They were offered conversion to Islam and in the alternative were made 'slaves', either to be sold in Arabian countries or forced to work as slaves to carry on the dirty menial work (like cleaning the latrines in the harems of the rulers). These came to be termed as 'untouchables'; their only fault was that they refused to accept Islam.

(c) Thus, there came to be several groups who bear the *'gotra'* of Brahmins and Kshatriyas, but as slaves they were forced to carry on menial jobs as untouchables. They are now called 'Scheduled Castes'. It may be noticed that all *"varna'* (so-called castes) according to Manu are *'karmana'* (by deed or profession) and not *'janmana'* (by birth). Reference may be had to the preface of the famous book by the noted Hindi writer Amrit Lal Nagar, *'Khub Nachayo Gopal'*.

20. So also the Scheduled Tribes. They left their hearths and homes and took refuge with their families in the jungle and became *'banbasies'*, rather then fall a prey to the invaders. Their long seclusion in the jungles from the normal life of Hindu faith resulted in these Scheduled Tribes. They still retain the Hindu Gods and customs.

IV. Minorities

21. These Scheduled Castes and Scheduled Tribes do not exist and could not exist among the so-called minorities, the Muslims and Christians. In fact the Muslims and Christians were a privileged class, when Muslim invaders and Christians ruled in India.

22. Articles 15 and 16 did not relate to minorities, who are dealt with in articles 29 and 30 of the Constitution (*see* draft Constitution). The Constituent Assembly amended the draft by deleting or substituting the word 'minority' in the draft in articles 15 and 16 by other words. There is nothing like 'Dalit Muslims' and 'Dalit Christians'. In theology *Kuran* and *Bible* consider all Muslims and Christians equal. There can be no social and educational backwardness among Muslims and Christians 'castes', as they do not exist there.

23. The Muslim and Christian invaders have been rulers and a privileged class in this country. The various reports including the report of Rangnath Mishra Commission characterized education among Christians as far above the average, being 80% to 90%, as against the average of 40% in some states. When Muslims and Christians were rulers, these so-called minorities had special privilege, they were granted special privileges in services and occupied important positions in the body politic of the country. It is absurd to characterize any section of Muslims or Christians educationally and socially backward as a class in India. The statute or notification and orders relating to them are based upon non-existent and imaginary facts and reasons.

24. Minorities have been defined in clause (c) of section 2 in the National Commission for Minorities Act, 1992, as meaning "a community notified as such by the Central Government". In fact this does not define a 'minority' as understood by the Constituent Assembly or the Constitution. It gives a blank cheque to the Government to notify any community as it pleases for that purpose. In fact definition is a legislative function of defining a constitutional concept and it cannot be delegated solely without laying down any guidelines. The whole definition is unconstitutional and gives unguided power to the Central Government to legislate or to define a 'minority' irrespective of what it meant to be Constituent Assembly at the time of framing of the Constitution, *vide*

In re *article 143, Constitution of India and Delhi Laws Act (1912)*, AIR 1951 SC 332: 1951 SCJ 527: 1951 SCR 747.

25. Supreme Court has held that the position for reservation has to be determined State-wise. Vide

***TMA Pai Foundation* v. *State of Karnataka*, (2002) 8 SCC 481: AIR 2003 SC 355: 2002 AIR SCW 4957.**

The State or Union (for some Union Territories) had no relevant material on which the Statutes, Rules or notifications regarding reservations are based. It did not appoint any commission for it and did not invite public opinion. The notification is based on politics of vote-banks or misinterpretation of reports and not on any relevant material before the Government; they are illegal and unconstitutional.

***T. Muralidhar Rao* v. *State of Andhra Pradesh*, 2004 (6) ALD 1.**

***B. Archana Reddy* v. *State of Andhra Pradesh*, 2005 (6) ALD 582: (2005) 6 ALT 6.**

26. That all such exceptions (from its very nature) were meant to be transitory and once their object is fulfilled, they cease to be operative. This is also further made clear by the spirit behind article 334 (special provisions). Thus these exceptions were transient, that is for the time being only and could not be elevated as a basic feature of the Constitution. This follows from their very object, the Constituent Assembly Debates, and the spirit behind article 334. Special provisions can exist for the purpose of advancement of socially and educationally backward class of citizens, so that persons constituting it, may join the mainstream, *vide* article 15(4). Reservation is provided for another backward class, which is not adequately represented in the services of the State, till they acquire such a place therein, *vide* article 16(4). The avowed purpose in the two cases is different. But when the object is achieved, there will no longer be any need for any special provisions or reservation. Expressing the same in dialectics, the object of special provision or reservation is to end them and give effect to the basic tenet of equality.

V. 'Class'

27. In case *'class'* is taken to mean caste, the transient nature of the provision regarding 'reservation' is lost, as caste inherited from father to son goes on. It can end only by repealing the enumeration of that caste in defining a 'class'.

28. 'Class' denotes a homogenous body. No heterogeneous body can be called a class.

(i) 'Muslims' and Christians are heterogeneous. So, they cannot be termed a 'class'.

(ii) The 'class' talked about in articles 15 and 16 are different. They cannot be clubbed or looked at together from the same angle. For this reason the relief talked about in article 16(4) is different than the relief in article 15(4). There is difference between 'reservation' and 'special provision' as the object is different.

29. The very fact that ***Indra Sawhney* v. *Union of India*, AIR 1993 SC 477: 1992 Supp SCC 217: 1902 AIR SCW 3682** suggests a 'creamy-layer' to be taken out shows that caste is not a homogeneous entity. Taking caste as a class is contrary to the Constitution.

30. The amendment of the article 15(4) added by the Constitutional 1[St] Amendment Act (or those added later) did not empower the Union of India to enact "The Central Educational Institutions (Reservation in Admission) Act, 2006 (Act No. 5 of 2007)".

VI. Question 3: Reservations in Elections

31. The Constitution provided for reservations in the Lok Sabha and the State Assemblies in paragraph 294 of the Draft Constitution, now article 332 of the Constitution. Reading the two clauses together is revealing. In the draft the reservation in the Legislature was suggested for Muslims and Indian Christians. There was a separate provision for Anglo-Indians, which is now not in vogue. When the division of India and creation of Pakistan became a settled fact the provision relating to reservation for minorities was deleted in the Constitution as passed. It may be mentioned that certain minorities like the Parsi Community, the Jews, the Jains and ultimately the Sikhs declined to have any reservation. A short provision was inserted for nomination of Anglo-Indian and Christian Community if they were not properly represented in the Lok Sabha or in the Legislative Assemblies in the State. The only reservation was retained for Scheduled Castes and Scheduled Tribes.

32. Constituencies initially elected two representatives, one representative was always to belong to the general category, while in reserved constituencies the other to the Scheduled Caste or to the Scheduled Tribe. Later on, when the constituencies came to elect a single representative, some were reserved for Scheduled Castes and some for Scheduled Tribes. There was no reservation for the so-called minorities. All reservation and special provisions were to cease after a period of 10 years (*vide* paragraph 305 of the draft constitution). This period was changed to 15 years by a constitutional amendment. Thereafter the Constitution has been amended under article 368 thereof, the latest being 'The Constitution (Ninety-seventh Amendment) Act, 2011', which has extended the period to 70 years.

33. Much water has flown down since ***Indra Sawhney's*** case. Now it is settled law that article 368 of the Constitution (the power to amend the Constitution) does not give a blank cheque to amend the Constitution in any way the legislature liked. It has ultimately been held that the basic feature or structure of the Constitution cannot be amended under article 368, *vide*

***Keshawanand Bharti* v. *State of Kerala,* (1973) 4 SCC 225 *see* p 1007: AIR 1973 SC 1461.**

***Indira Nehru Gandhi* v. *Raj Narain,* AIR 1975 SC 1590: (1975) 2 SCC 159.**

***I.R. Coelho* v. *State of Tamil Nadu,* (2007) 2 SCC 1 (111, 112): AIR 2007 SC 861 (892-93): 2007 AIR SCW 611.**

34. 'Equality' before the law being a basic feature of the Constitution, there can be no amendment changing that basic feature. In other words, all citizens are equal before the law; there can be no reservation in favour of any particular caste or religious group. Thus, reservation could not be introduced by an amendment by addition of the word 'reservation' in article 15(4). Now it is axiomatic that what could not be done directly, cannot be done indirectly by putting an interpretation on words 'special provisions' used therein. The interpretation supposed to be put in ***Indra Sawhney's*** case is void in the light of the law now laid down relating to article 368 of the Constitution.

35. As noted above, article 368 of the Constitution did not empower the Parliament to amend any basic feature of the Constitution. The right to equality being a basic feature of the Constitution and reservation being contrary to it, the amendments for reservation were beyond the power granted by article 368 of the Constitution and *ultra vires*. The amendments in the true light were made to appease certain sections of the society and were *ultra vires*. The result is that there can now be no reservation in the elections and the ninety-seventh amendment must be declared invalid.

36. Similarly articles 343D and 343T inserted in Part IX by The Constitution (Seventy-third Amendment) Act, 1992 and 243-ZJ (1) Second Proviso by The Constitution (Ninety-Seventh Amendment) Act, 2011 are unconstitutional. It may be further mentioned that a co-operative society is a voluntary organisation of like persons for co-operation in a particular field. There may not be any Scheduled Caste or Scheduled Tribe or woman among the members. The provision providing for reservation in the Board of management in the co-operative society, in which there is no such member, runs counter to the basic idea of a co-operative society.

37. Reservation in a single post of chairman of a local body is further invalid as it amounts to disenfranchising a certain section of the society to stand for the post of the Chairman. So for as the membership of the Lok Sabha and the State Assembly is concerned it may be noted that a citizen can stand for membership of the Lok Sabha from any Parliamentary constituency in the country and a citizen of the State can stand for membership from any constituency of the State Assembly provided he fulfilled the requisite conditions for it. But a citizen enrolled as a voter in a particular urban area cannot stand for the Chairmanship of any other urban area. Thus, a reservation in the post of Chairmanship of an urban area precludes him for standing for the post of the Chairmanship at all. It is against the basic feature of democracy and is invalid. The law has wrongly created a fiction of grouping all the posts of chairmanship in the State together. The fiction is contrary to the fundamental feature and amounts to fraud on the Constitution. For the aforesaid reason also, the reservation for the post of any Chairman in local bodies is *ultra vires*.

VII. The Position Now

38. The Supreme Court had held earlier before article 15(4) was amended by first constitutional amendments that reservation was unconstitutional, *vide*—

***State of Madras* v. *Smt. Champakam Dorairajan*, 1951 SCJ 313: 1951 SCR 525: AIR 1951 SC 226 paras 8, 11, upholding AIR (38) 1951 Mad 120 (FB).**

39. In view of the latest pronouncements of the Supreme Court, the amendments being *otiose* or invalid, the position of the above case revives. Thus all reservations except that existed initially are invalid on this group also.

40. Moreover it is settled law that if a power is granted under the law (the same is true of the Constitution), it must be exercised within a reasonable time, or not at all. The exercise of the power is lost by efflux of unreasonable time and has to be declared *otiose*.

***Ibrahimpatnam Taluk Vyavasaya Coolie Sangham v. K. Suresh Reddy*, AIR 2003 SC 3592: 2003 AIR SCW 4084: (2003) 7 SCC 667 paras 12, 13, 19, 20.**

***State of Himachal Pradesh* v. *Rajkumar Brijender Singh*, AIR 2004 SC 3218: 2004 AIR SCW 3168: (2004) 10 SCC 585 (para 6).**

***S.B. Gurbaksh Singh* v. *Union of India*, AIR 1976 SC 1115: (1976) 3 SCR 247: (1976) 2 SCC 181 para 15(b)** as further explained in the aforesaid two cases.

41. Reservations were temporary exceptions and the power to create new exceptions amounts to a law counter to basic feature of equality and is now unreasonable (60 years after coming into force of the Constitution). It is a sad commentary that even after 62 years, we have not been able to cure the deficiency for which the reservation was meant. There must be something radically wrong with the policy pursued. The power if it existed must be taken now to be non-existent. Further the continuance of previous reservation has become *otiose* and its exercise is not warranted by the Constitution. It is unreasonable and hit by article 14 thereof. The Constitution does not empower any legislature to enact an unreasonable law, as that would be discriminatory. Article 14 of the Constitution applies to legislature also.

CHAPTER 2

Changing the Colour of 'Secularism'

1. The political parties put on their own hue on 'secularism'. But it is strange to find the Supreme Court of India imposing an unwarranted colour of its own on the concept, while supposedly construing article 27 of the Constitution. It is said, the courts do not legislate, they only interpret the law. But here is an example of personal predilections of judges thrusting another colour the language was incapable of bearing. The whole background of freedom struggle, the reasons that inspired the Constituent Assembly to frame that article and the tragedy of partition, which went to shape the Constitution are forgotten and thrown away. Their place has been taken by a mere *ipse dixit* of the Judges without any discussion. The recent decision of the Supreme Court, ***Prafulla Garodia*** **v.** ***Union of India*****, (2011) 2 SCC 568,** cannot be supported by any canon of interpretation.

2. 'Secularism' means a 'divorce between the State and religion'. The word came into vogue in the beginning of nineteenth century when the scientific developments had made deep inroads into religious beliefs and the attendance in the Church had declined, so were its revenues. This put the idea in the minds of religious leaders that they should draw some programme for 'secular' or non-religious activities to attract their 'flock'. It was in this context, with the attempt of the Church to enter into non-religious area that the word acquired a meaning.

3. The Supreme Court quoted article 27 of the Constitution, which mandated: "No person shall be compelled to pay any taxes, the proceeds of which are specifically appropriated in payment of expenses for the promotion of any particular religion or religious denomination".

The meaning is apparent; it, *inter alia,* prohibits appropriation by the State of any amount from the Consolidated Fund of the State towards 'the maintenance of any particular religion or religious denomination'.

4. A series of decisions of the Supreme Court have established that religious rites and practices are a part of religion, *vide*

***His Holiness Srimad Perarulala Ethiraja Ramanuja Jeeyar Swami* v. *State of Tamil Nadu,* (1972) 3 SCR 815: 1973 (1) SCJ 346: AIR 1972 SC 1586 (para 12):**

The (rulings of) the Supreme Court have placed the main principles underlying the provisions (relating to religion) beyond controversy. The *first* is that protection of these articles is not limited to matters of doctrine or belief, they extend also to acts done in pursuance of religion and therefore contain the guarantee for rituals and observances, ceremonies and modes of worship, which are integral part of religion. "The *second* is that what constitutes an essential part of a religion or religious practices has to be decided by the courts with reference to the doctrine of particular religion and includes practices which are regarded by the community as a part of its religion. ..."

5. The words are borrowed from the decision in ***Commissioner Hindu Religious Endowments* v. *Sri Lakshmindra Tirtha Swamiar of Sri Shirur Mutt,* AIR 1954 SC 282: 1954 SCJ 335: 1954 SCR 1005** and other cases, where it was held that the acts done in pursuance of religious belief are a part of religion. Further it is said,

> "A religion may not only lay down a code of ethical rules for its followers to accept, it might prescribe rituals and observances, ceremonies and modes of

worship which are regarded as integral parts of religion and these forms and observances might extend even to matter of food and dress".

6. 'Haj' is an integral part of Muslim religion, which enjoins every Muslim to undertake the pilgrimage with religious rites and practices to Makka. Furthermore, non-Muslims are strictly prohibited from taking part in it. Article 27 prohibits the State from spending any part of the Consolidated Fund of the State in payment of expenses 'for the promotion or maintenance of any particular religion'. The question therefore is whether the Haj subsidy by the government is promotion or maintenance of Islam. Haj being admittedly one of the five fundamental tenets of Islam is the Haj subsidy promotes it or is money spent in promotion or maintenance of religion?

7. The article is an injunction against utilization of Consolidated Fund of the State for payment of expenses in promotion or maintenance of any religious activity. It postulates a fundamental right of every citizen that he cannot be compelled to pay any taxes, the proceeds of which are specifically appropriated in payment of expenses for the promotion or maintenance of any particular religion or religious denomination. As a corollary the State cannot use the taxpayers' money as assistance in a religious activity.

8. The Court noticed the leading case of Commissioner, HRE (*supra*), yet without analyzing it and without any reason in law, the Court jumped to the conclusion as follows:

> "There can be two views about article 27. One view can be that article 27 is attracted only when the statute by which the tax is levied specifically states that the proceeds of the tax will be utilized for a particular religion. The other view can be that article 27 will be attracted even when the statute is a general statute, like the Income Tax Act or the Central Excise Act or the State Sales Tax statutes (which do not specify for what purpose the proceeds will be utilized) provided that a substantial part of such proceeds are in fact utilized for a particular religion." (*Emphasis by the Court.*)

9. The last portion (the proviso) is an unwarranted gloss put by the Court. After the partition of India when the Constituent Assembly met to pass finally this article, a Muslim member moved an amendment by insertion of the words 'wholly or partly' at the appropriate place. The amendment was rejected on the ground that the 'whole' included a 'part' in legal parlance. The gloss is a figment of imagination and is directly contrary to the ruling.

10. It will be noticed that general statutes impose taxes, while the appropriation of funds is usually by various Appropriation Acts. 'Secularism' has been held to be a basic feature of our Constitution, as also noted in its Preamble. The State cannot act in the aid of any religious practice, as secularism envisages a separation (in the words of the Supreme Court of USA, a 'divorce') between the State and religion.

11. The leading case on the import of article 27 of the Constitution is,—***Commissioner HRE Endowment* v. *Sri Lakshammdra Tirth,*** (*supra*): The court held

> *"What is forbidden by this article is the specific appropriation of proceeds of any tax in payment of expenses for the promotion or maintenance of any particular religion or religious denomination. The reason underlying this provision is obvious. Ours being a secular state and there being freedom of religion guaranteed by the Constitution, both to the individuals and to groups, it is against the policy of the Constitution to pay out of public funds any money for the promotion or maintenance of any particular religion or denomination."*

The question again arose in ***Sri Devi Kodandram Asharam* v. *State of Andhra Pradesh,* (1997) 4 SCC 189 (page 197)**:

> *"Article 27 of the Constitution prohibits spending of any expenses for promotion or maintenance of particular religion or religious denomination from out of the funds flowing from the public exchequer."*

12. Distinction is also drawn between religious and secular activities in article 25(2). In ***S.R. Bommai* v. *Union of***

***India*, AIR 1994 SC 1918: 1994 AIR SCW 2946: (1994) 3 SCC 1,** the Judges ruled as follows:

Ahmadi J. (para 24-end to 25, 28)

> *"article 27 provides that no person shall be compelled to pay any taxes the proceed whereof are specifically appropriated in payment of expenses for the promotion and maintenance of any particular religion. It means that the State revenue cannot be utilized for the promotion of any religion or religious group"*

PB Sawant & Kuldip Singh JJ: (page 2000 column II),

> *"These provisions by implication prohibit the establishment of a theocratic State and prevent the State either identifying itself with or favouring any particular religion or religious sect."* (*See* also K Ramaswami J: paras 114-24. BP Jeewan Reddy J paras 236-237).

In ***Bal Patil* v. *Union of India*, AIR 2005 SC 3172: 2005 AIR SCW 3762: (2005) 6 SCC 690 (para 37),** it is said *'The basic principle of secularism is separation between the Church and the State'.*

13. William O' Douglas J in his Tagore Law Lecture, 'Studies in American and Indian Constitutional Law' has described how people of different faiths even those persecuted for their religious beliefs (including renegades and rebels from the orthodox church) of different races and speaking different toungues took refuge in America (USA) and how their Constitution welded them into a nation. They had brought with them stories of religious persecution they had suffered. (And who does not know the harrowing tales of atrocities and tyranny committed on the innocent, peaceful and law abiding people in the name of religion by foreign rulers in India.) Douglas J, talking of this marvel, says 'one is the manner in which she (America) built one community and one people out of many races'. America's creed is expressed in the First Amendment to their Constitution, "The Congress shall make no law respecting establishment of religion or prohibiting the free exercise thereof...."

14. The experience in India is the same, including peoples of different races seeking refuge in India to escape religious tyranny at the hands of the priesthood of the ruling class from olden days. At the recent times of living memory, why forget the holocaust and the exodus in the wake of great tragedy of partition. It is alleged, there was a hundred miles long procession from Pakistan to India with bag and baggage on the back and tiny tots on their shoulders. Why forget the more recent events, the plight of Kashmiri Pandits hounded from their hearths and homes in their own valley. And there has been a constant trickle from Bangladesh. For whose sin (?) one asks in vain. It is in this background and the Constituent Assembly debates the reason and the meaning of article should be sought

15. Experience of religious tyranny being similar, although of a small scale compared to what overwhelmed India, let us see how the Supreme Court of USA dealt with this problem. How the separation of the Church and the State was worked out?

16. In ***Illinois* v. *Board of Education,* (1947) 82 Law Ed 649: 333 US 203** that Court asserted:

> "No tax of any amount, large or small, can be used to support any religious activities, whatever they may be called or whatsoever form they may adopt. ... Neither the State nor the Federal Government can, openly or secretly, participate in the affairs of any religious organisation or groups or *vice versa*. In the words of Jefferson 'the clause against establishment of religion by law' was intended to erect a wall of separation between the Church and the State. ..."
>
> "(This) does not manifest a governmental hostility to religion. A manifestation of such hostility could be at war with our national tradition as embodied in the First Amendment guaranteeing the free exercise of religion for the First Amendment rest upon the premise that both religion and Government each best work to achieve their lofty aims, if each is left free from other within its respective spheres. Or that it has erected a

wall between Church and State, which need be kept high and impregnable."

"Here not only are the State's tax supported school buildings used for dissemination of religions doctrines, the State also affords sectarian groups invaluable aids in that it helps to provide peoples for their religious classes though use of the State's compulsory public school machinery. This is not separation of Church and State."

"(There) are consequences not amenable to statistics. But they are precisely the consequences against which the Constitution was directed, when it prohibited the Government, common to all, from becoming embroiled, however innocently, in the destructive religious conflicts of which the history of even this country records some dark pages. ... We renew our conviction that we have staked the very existence of our country on the faith that complete separation between the State and religion is best for State and best for religion"

17. The recent landmark judgment of that court is ***Lemon* v. *Kurtzman*, (1971) 29 Law Ed (2nd series) 745**. It says, *inter alia*, (*vide* head note 4)

> "In determining the constitutionality under the prohibition against a law respecting an establishment of religion, the court must draw lines with reference to three main evils against which the establishment clause was intended to afford protection that is, sponsorship, financial support, and active involvement of the sovereign in religious activity." [This remarkable judgment should be read as a whole].

18. The judgment of our Supreme Court refers to the question of *Melas*. The State gives no aid for any (so-called Hindu) religious *Melas*. The arrangement for Magh or Kumbh *Mela* is made under UP *Melas* Act, 1938. The Government used to impose a pilgrim tax for it till recently. Under section 6 of the Act, the District Magistrate is empowered to impose tolls and fees. Under section 7, the District Magistrate can prescribe rent for the sites and also for market places, religions, societies etc. A provision is also made for recovery of rent under section 14 as arrear of land revenue. Moreover no permanent structure can be built in the area. The Government actually earns revenue from the Kumbh and the Magh *Mela*. The so-called (Hindu) *Tirth* and *Melas* are different from religious activities of Islam or proselytizing religions. Everybody is free to visit these without taking part in any religious ceremony. They are in fact national fairs free for all citizens and even Muslims and Christians with foreigners take part in it, often taking a holy dip at the Sangam. Nobody is forced to participate in any religious activity there.

19. Then there is the strange hackneyed argument: "There is no violation of articles 14 and 15 because facilities are also given and expenditure incurred by the Government for other religions." The Supreme Court of USA in ***Plessy* v. *Ferguson*, (1896) 41 Law Ed 356: 163 US 537** blessed the formula of 'separate but equal facilities in segregation' as not contravening the equality clause. It took 58 years for that court in *Brown* v. *Board of Education of Topeka*, (99 Law Ed 1083) to realize just the opposite, "Allegedly equal but separate facilities are necessarily unequal." How many years more our Supreme Court will take to realize this universal truth?

20. And what about section 32 clause (ii) of Haj Committee Act (Central Act 35 of 2002)? The challenge to that Act is noted in the very beginning as the main contention. Yet there is not a whisper about it in the judgment. Is it because it throws overboard the reasoning in it? And why this basic issue of constitutional law not referred to the Constitution Bench?

21. Look at the countries of proselytizing religions. The Christian world had for fourteen centuries the Holy Roman Empire. The Muslim world, since the very inception of Islam had the 'Caliphate', thrown overboard after the First World War. All powers were concentrated then in the religious head. On the other hand, India is the birthplace of the republics *(gana-tantra)*. In his famous book *'The Hindu Polity'* Dr. Kashi

Prasad Jaiswal described 3000 years of republican rule before the Christian era. Many ideas of alleged monarchial rule, for example of the time of Chatrapati Shivaji (*see* the last chapter of that book), were borrowed from these republics. India was never a theocratic state (except under foreign rulers, when *'padshahi'* held the sway) in the sense used in the rest of the world.

22. Hinduism is not a 'religion'. Normal meaning of 'dharm' in Sanskrit is 'law'. (That is why Manu called his book on Jurisprudence as *'Dharma-shashtra'*.) 'Hindutva' is in fact 'Indian-ness', the secular way of social life in India as interpreted by our Supreme Court in ***Shastri Yagnapurushdasji* v. *Muldas*, 1966 (2) SCJ 502: (1966) 3 SCR 242: AIR 1966 SC 1119 (para 27 to 40); *Commissioner of Wealth Tax* v. *R. Sridharan*, 1976 Supp SCR 478: (1976) 4 SCC 489 (paras 10, 16, 23) and *Ramesh Yashwant Prabhoo Dr.* v. *Prabhakar Kashinath Kunte*, AIR 1996 SC 1113: 1996 AIR SCW 652: (1996) 1 SCC 130 (paras 32-45).** We cannot understand the ethos of Bharat without bearing in mind this essential historical difference. The western countries teaching us 'secularism' is like bringing coal to Newcastle.

23. The interpretation put by the Supreme Court reminds me of the famous dissent of Lord Atkin in ***Liversidge* v. *Anderson*, 1942 AC 206: (1941) 3 All ER 338: 116 LT 1** (page 361 bottom). Said Lord Atkin: "I know of only one authority which might justify the suggested method of construction. 'When I use a word,' Humpty Dumpty said in rather a scornful tone, 'it means just what I choose it to mean, neither more nor less.' 'The question is, said Alice, 'whether you can make words mean different things.' 'The question is', said Humpty Dumpty, 'which is to be the master—that's all.' (Alice Through the Looking Glass C.)."

24. It has the seed of fragmentation and divisiveness on religious lines. It sharpens the consciousness of differences. There are unforeseen consequences, precisely those against which the Constitution was directed, when it prohibited the State common to all from dabbling with religious matters and 'becoming embroiled however innocently in the destructive conflict of religious dogmas of which history records some dark pages'. The Court abandoned the rule of purposive interpretation to substitute it with half baked ideas.

25. Let the quintessence of our forefathers, who forged a nation out of diverse faiths and religious denominations dawn upon our judiciary. Let it eschew catch phrases and populist slogans and concentrate upon the ideas that permeated the freedom struggle and reason behind the particular provision of the Constitution – what inspired the cream of Society assembled as the Constituent Assembly in the background of events that led to the great tragedy of partition of the motherland.

CHAPTER 3

'Gotra' and the 'Khap Panchayat' Agitation

1. A truism is often repeated in law 'He knoweth not the law, who knoweth not the reason thereof'. The recent controversy generated by the 'Khap Panchayat' agitation is an illustration of it.

2. The ancient Indian society practiced the rule of exogamy, that is marriage outside one's fold and consanguine or near relations. It is based on two-fold reason. First is physiological. Marriage between near blood relations results in weak progeny or genetic degradation. The children sometimes may suffer from deformation, mental disability or haemophilia and the like. It is alleged that Pharaon kings of Egypt ultimately became extinct as they inter-married inside their family. They had a false notion of purity of blood. The prohibition of marriages of two persons related to each other as '*sapinda*' under the Hindu Law arose from physiological considerations for the well-being of the race.

3. Then there are sociological considerations for the taboo on certain marriages. A cultural or religious custom or values prohibited marriage between persons ordinarily having unrestricted or frequent access to each other in life. It required self-control ('*sainyam*' in Sanskrit) and sublimation of relations in life. This is necessary to secure the even tenure of social life in the family or the neighbourhood. The Hindu tradition of tying '*rakshabandhan*' (a piece of thread) on the wrist of another, thus creating a bond as brother and sister is one such example. The prohibition of marriage between persons belonging the same *'gotra'* or *'pravar'* or marriage of persons of different castes (*'varna'* in Sanskrit) emanated from social considerations. But the words *'gotra'* (or *'pravar'*) or *'varna'* have undergone a sea-change during the foreign rule.

4. Etymologically *'gotra'* denoted shelter for a herd of cows ('go' = cow and 'tra' is a suffix meaning a shelter). The primary meaning of *'gotra'* was a *'goshala'* (cowshed). The *'ashrams'* had their *'gurukul'* (family of the preceptor), where his pupils (students) resided. The *'gurukul'* invariably maintained a *'goshala'*, looked after by the students. The cows used to be donated by the general public and the parents and guardians of students residing there. Thus, the *'gurukul'* or the family of preceptor, so to speak, was a *'gotra'*. The pupils came to be known by the name of its preceptor and took over his name as their *'gotra'*.

5. The social order in ancient times was based on what was known as *'ashram'* or *'gurukul'* system. A child when he reached the schooling age was sent to an *'ashram'* presided over by a *'rishi'* (sage or supreme teacher). These *'ashrams'* were residential seats of learning, which not only educated their pupils in the modern sense but imparted *'sanskars'* (religions or ethical rules and values of society). Since both boys and girls and young members of both sex lived in the *'ashram'*, it was necessary to prohibit marriage between persons reading in the same *'ashram'*. It was to instill self-restraint or *'brahmacharya'*, sublimation of their desires and discipline of *'chhatra-dharm'* in their lives to enable them to devote themselves exclusively to their studies and acquire the qualities, which would make them a useful unit of the society. The taboo primarily extended to all the inmates of the same *'ashram'* or *'gurukul'* residing there. It did not extend to their children, unless they were inmates of one and the same *'ashram'* or *'gurukul'* at the same time.

6. In the *'ashram'* the preceptor and his pupils lived together as a family. It was named after the *'rishi'*, who presided over it and was the *'kulpati'* or supreme preceptor. The pupils residing or living in his *'ashram'* were, so to speak, his children. They together formed the family of the *'ashram'* and thus got one *'gotra'*, named after their preceptor. They were considered to be brothers and sisters. The prohibition relating to *inter se* marriage governed them. It may be mentioned that *'gotraj'* or *'goti'* in Hindi means a person of the same village, locality or vicinity.

7. The original *'ashram'* or *'rishi'* (sage) are said to be eight in number, who manned the original eight 'ashram' or centres of learning. They are Agastya Atri, Bharadwaj, Gautam, Jamadagni, Kashyap, Vasistha and Vishwamitra (often figuratively spoken of as progenitors of the human race). They gave rise to *'gotra'*, which bear their name. In course of time there came other *'rishis'* who started their own subsidiary 'ashram' affiliated or attached to one or more of original eight *'rishis'*. The word 'I' means 'superior' or 'senior'. What was meant by *'pravar'* is not clear; usually the word is used in a sense akin to *'gotra'*. Golapchander Sircar says the *'pravar'* is named after the three male ancestors of the aforesaid *'rishis'*. Probably the word meant to denote the *'gotra'* of the 'ashram', to which the subsidiary 'ashram' was affiliated or attached and propagated its teachings.

8. Similarly the word *'varna'* (or caste in modern parlance). Manu in his *'Dharm-shastra'* (*'Manu-smriti'*) says, "All persons are born *'shudras'*. When they entered the *'ashram'* (for schooling), their aptitude and capabilities were tested. A pupil was educated and trained in the task most suited to him." Gita says God has divided mankind according to their qualities and the profession (*guna-karma vibhagshah*). The *varna* that was assigned to him, according to Manu, was *'karmana'*, by the deeds and profession and not by birth (*'janmana'*). Plato in his book 'Republic' talks of the four functions of the State. The Greeks borrowed their idea of republic from *'gantantra'*, the republics of ancient India. The tasks spoken of by him are a reflection of the four *'varna'* of Manu. "Thus", says Manu "a child born of a *'shudra'* father, if his qualities and potentiality is that of a Brahmin, got that *'varna'* and like education". In ordinary course he married a similarly educated spouse.

9. These *'ashrams'* or seats of learning became a target and thus first casualty of a foreign invasion. The story from Takshila in the Northwest to Nalanda in the East is the same. After *ashrams* were uprooted and erased from the map of the country, the *'varna'* gradually became by birth (*'janmana'*), The child was presumed to adopt the father's profession and usually took it, as he grew in the surroundings of his family. Thus the, conception of *'varna'* as well as *'gotra'* changed from *'karma'* (deeds or profession) to *'janma'* (birth). So also *'gotra'* became hereditary.

10. Traditions of a nation or society can only be evaluated of its peaceful existence. Various aberrations enter the society when there is foreign invasion or war. Then the only idea, which dominates, is to repulse the aggression. During the Second World War various laws and rules were made, which sound irrational if one forgets the existence of war. These rules may survive even after the war has ended as aberrations or mal-practices or wrong customs (*'kureeti'*). India has suffered from foreign invasion or rule in one part or the other for nearly a thousand years. That aggression still survives in the form of remnants of a foreign rule all over the country and in the form of mental slavery. The *'ashram'* institutions were gradually wiped out during the period of the struggle in one part of the other.

11. Unfortunately some controversy has arisen regarding *'Manu-Smriti'* because of interpolations made in later years. For the original text, some research edition (especially by Arya Samajists) may be consulted. The institutes of Manu have to be interpreted in the light of its purpose or reason behind it. More so, as there have been later interpolations to suit particular anomalous situation and some became otiose or unmeaning in the present context.

12. With the *'ashram'* and its *'gurukul'* having become extinct for long, the reason behind the prohibition of *'sagotra'* marriages (in the same *'gotra'*) is no longer valid. Even the original concept of *'gotra'* has disappeared. It is now reckoned by birth has lost its meaning except for some religious rights. Instead customs developed, under which a marriage is avoided in the same village or locality or within a particular radius of it, say 10 kilometres or ten villages round about, as a substitute for it. Indeed the *'sagotra'* marriage became common by avoiding marriage between persons residing in the neighbouring villages or vicinities. Under the Hindu Law custom overrides the written text of law. Such marriages were therefore valid. The clarificatory legislation was enacted in the name of 'The Hindu Marriage Disabilities Removal Act, 1946'. It provided that notwithstanding any text or interpretation of Hindu Law or custom or usage, no marriage, which was otherwise valid would be invalid only because parties belonged to the same *'gotra'*.

13. Similarly caste or *'varna'* has lost its original meaning. The marriage of persons belonging to different castes came to be recognized by a series of legislation. Marriages between Arya Samajists came to be recognized by the Arya Marriage Validation Act, 1937. It was declared that no such marriage would be deemed ever to have been invalid merely because the parties at any time belonged to different castes, or sub-castes or either or both before their marriage belonged to a religion other than Hinduism. Thus, such distinctions never invalidated an otherwise valid Hindu marriage.

14. Then was enacted the Hindu Marriage Act, 1956. Belonging to the same *gotra* is not a disqualification for marriage therein also. There are in this connection two conditions for a Hindu marriage, the parties should not be related as *'sapinda'* of each other and should not be prohibited relations. The *'gotra'* is no longer relevant. These two prohibitions correspond to the two reasons (the physiological and sociological) referred to above.

15. The law member of the Government of India Justice B.N. Rau, who was entrusted with the task of framing the Hindu Code had said, "It is not for me to amend the Hindu Law. My task is to codify it as our *'Rishis'* and *'Munis'* had laid down." But in one respect there is a departure, probably introduced by amendment of the original draft. Manu defined this prohibition in Manusmriti (5/60) "*Sapinda* relationship ceases with the seventh generation and the connection is broken." The Hindu Marriage Act prescribes that *'sapinda'* relation ceases (counting the person concerned as the first generation) with the third generation (inclusive) in the line of ascent from the mother and in the fifth generation (inclusive) in the line of ascent from the father. According to modern genetic hereditary science, the potentialities of deleterious disorders of inbreeding end with the seventh generation. This reaffirms the institute of Manu. The *'Khap Panchayat'* is probably right in insisting on a larger degree of this relationship.

16. But this alone does not solve their problem. Their problem of sons or daughters running away and marrying or living together as husband and wife or securing court orders for it is a social problem. Probably there is no legal solution for it. The solution lies in giving them *'sanskars'* with love and affection at home for sublimation and a chaste life devoted to values and ideals of society, as we understand. The modern schools do not carry this task of ancient *'ashrams'*. It is no use running after will-of-the-wisp of *'gotra'*. Social sanction of marriage outside the immediate vicinity has to be built.

CHAPTER 4

The Story Retold

I

1. Sometimes a month or two after that fateful day (namely 06-12-1992) Prof. B.R. Grover (erstwhile Chairman of the Indian Council of Historical Research) met me. He told me of an incident as reported to him by his near relative, who was close to Sri P.V. Narasimha Rao, the then Prime Minister of India. He told me that his relative had an appointment to meet the Prime Minister in the afternoon of that fateful day. Having reached a little early, he was told, as he sat in the ante-room, that the Prime Minister was having his afternoon siesta and would be coming out shortly. The Prime Minister had kept himself abreast of the happenings in Ayodhya before he went to take the nap. As soon as the Prime Minister came inside the room, the Secretary monitoring the happenings told him that the structure had fallen down. The Prime Minister ejaculated *"Chalo, Bharat ka kalank door hua"* (Well, the disgrace of Bharat has been washed off). He told Prof. Grover, "It stuck in my mind as an echo of millions of our countrymen."

II

2. I had been taken to Ayodhya on 05-12-1992 by the then Law Minister Sri Om Prakash Singh to address a gathering of holymen of the 'Marg Darshak Mandal' and others, guiding the Ayodhya movement. That meeting had been called under the aegis of Vishwa Hindu Parishad, who desired me to address them regarding the stay order passed by the

High Court, so that its total compliance be assured; and the orders of the Court be not violated. We started from Lucknow after lunch and reached Ayodhya in the afternoon. I was required to address the gathering of prominent workers of the Vishwa Hindu Parishad and the *'sadhu-sant'* at the helm of the movement. I informed them about the interim order of the Court, which had been passed in the writ petitions challanging the acquisition of 2.77 acres near about the disputed structure, leaving the barricaded portion intact. The disputed structure and its courtyards and immediate vicinity or the way to it were not affected by this acquisition. It may be mentioned that we were not concerned with the structure and the inner and the outer courtyards and the land near about, which had been enclosed by an iron barricade.

3. After the whole position had been clarified and questions answered, it was decided and meeting resolved that the *kar-sewaks* (workers) would form a people's chain to take water and sand from the Saryu River up to the platform previously built for discourses. This platform existed at a distance from the structure and its immediate vicinity, outside the barricade and had nothing to do with it. The consensus arrived at in my presence was that Court's orders would be obeyed in letter and spirit and no construction would be made. The only activity that would be carried out was to rub the platform with sand and water by the *kar-sewaks*. This was required to prepare it for building later a *'go-puram'* (main entrance). It was for a while till the decision of the writ petitions, when stay order would lapse. Neither the writ petitions, nor the workers of Vishwa Hindu Parishad or the Marg Darshak Mandal or *kar-sewaks* assembled there had anything to do with the structure or land enclosed by the protective iron barricade erected by the Government.

4. The strangest part of this interim order passed in the Writ Petition No. 3540 of 1991, ***Mohd. Hashim* v. *State of Uttar Pradesh,*** relating to acquisition of 3.77 acres of land was that no Muslim was affected, whether the writ petition was allowed or dismissed. If allowed and acquisition quashed, the land would have reverted to its former owners. The Ram

Janmabhumi Nyas held more than 80% of the land acquired, the remaining being occupied by minor temples or squatters. This would have enabled the Nyas to begin reconstruction of the temple on its own land. In case, writ petitions were dismissed and acquisition upheld, the Government of U.P. could grant a piece of land unconnected with the structure to begin the construction of the Temple or construction of Sri Lakshman Temple, which was underway when acquisition was made. No Muslim had any say, nor was in possession of the acquired land at any time. Had the writ petitions been decided, the structure and the land inside the barricade would not have been touched. Constant efforts were made to get the writ petition decided but all in vain.

III

5. Long after I was required to argue the case of Criminal Revision No. 255 of 1997, ***Rajmata Vijay Raje Sindhiya* v. *State of Uttar Pradesh,*** before the Lucknow Bench of the Allahabad High Court. This case was connected with several other revisions. I had then occasion to scrutinise the Police record, including statements made by witnesses examined by the Central Bureau of Investigation (CBI) under section 173(5) Cr.P.C. a composite challan had been filed in Crime Nos. 197/1992 and 198/1992 along with 47 reports of media persons. Jagdish Bhalla J, by his order dated 12-2-2001, quashed the proceedings taken in respect of Crime No. 198/1992 as being without jurisdiction. He also set aside the orders of the Special Judge (CBI) so far as they related to it. The judgment is reported at 2001 Cr LJ 1765.

6. Let us reconstruct the events of that fateful day and its background. The Police papers coupled with video films, which escaped destruction during the assault of what has been called by me as the second wave as it entered the barricade round the structure and its precincts, reveal a picture.

7. It may be mentioned that the *kar-sewaks* called by Vishwa Hindu Parishad were to come from outside Uttar Pradesh especially from the south. It had directed that no worker from Uttar Pradesh would take part in the *kar-sewa* except local workers who had to make arrangements for the *kar-sewaks*. Arrangements had to be made for the gathering in this connection, including the supply of water for which tanks had to be carried by ropes to the top of Kuber Tila to ensure supply of clean drinking water to places where *kar-sewaks* were lodged. (It is ridiculous to find that after demolition of the structure some persons showed their ire by labelling it as a preparation for it.)

8. The State Government had got the structure with its precincts completely barricaded by iron fences. It had further built a wall beyond the acquired area to ensure safety from assault from the sloping backside. A contingent of Provincial Armed Constabulary was stationed there for security of the structure. A few days before the date for *kar-sewa* arrived, the Union Government sent, without consent of the State Government or prior information to it, a big contingent of para-military forces.

9. This Central Reserve Police Force came from the South, unacquainted with the local language. They were deployed here from Karnataka, Andhra Pradesh and, it is said, even Tamil Nadu. The *kar-sewaks* had also come from outside, mostly from the South. A posse of about a thousand *kar-sewaks* came from the constituency of Sri P.V. Narasimha Rao in Andhra Pradesh. The contingent of Central Para-military Forces completely displaced the U.P. Provincial Armed Constabulary and took over the security arrangement on the spot. (Why blame the State Government for any security lapse?). The Uttar Pradesh Government had sent a protest, but in vain.

10. From the police documents (if we disabuse our minds of exaggerations and of freak or purposive statements) a picture emerges of the incident. At about 9:30 or 10:00 a.m. some *kar-sewaks* tried to enter the barricade. I know that Rashtriya Swayam-Sewak Sangh (RSS) volunteers of Ayodhya had been directed to keep a watch, so that no *kar-sewak* went near the barricade. These volunteers tried to dissuade the *kar-sewaks* (they were from the South), but there was the language problem. So Sri H.V. Sheshadri (*Sar-karyavah* of the RSS), who hailed from Karnataka and knew not only all the South Indian but several other languages of the country, repeatedly appealed to the *kar-sewaks* on public delivery system in several languages to desist from going near or inside the barricade. He also asked the volunteers to request the *kar-sewaks* not to go to that side. Sri L.K. Advani and other BJP leaders also made such appeals. The *kar-sewaks* were persuaded not to enter or go near the barricade. Some of the appeals were recorded by the videography at the place from where directions were being given to the *kar-sewaks*.

11. At about 11 AM, there came another wave, allegedly with saffron scarfs tied on their heads. The group composing the second wave did not want themselves to be photographed or exposed to video recording. They protested against it and when the persons with the video and other cameras insisted on taking photographs, they forced the films or recordings open and destroyed them. When some media-persons still persisted, they went even to the extent of destroying their equipment.

12. Who were these men, who did not want to be known or photographed? And could enter the barricade manned by para-military forces from the South so easily? The assault/aggression against media persons points to the fact that the aggressors wanted their identity to remain hidden. The conduct of genuine *kar-sewaks,* who had come to Ayodhya from far off places for *kar-sewa,* showed that they perceived themselves as heroes or soldiers of 'Lord Ram'. Why would they, in the first place, try to hide their identity. They were acting on the call of conscience. If the intention were to loot the photographic implements, why would they break the equipment in the first place rendering it unusable. The police investigation avoided unearthing the identity of people comprising the second wave.

13. There appears one hypothesis, which can explain the facts. The people comprising the second wave might have been a part of the Central Reserve Police from the southern States (out of a third kept in reserve), who wanted to keep their identity hidden and secret. Further they could communicate with the Central forces in their own language and thus gain easy access inside the barricade to the structure.

14. It may be that some *kar-sewaks* from the South had occasion to talk to Central Reserve Police personnel in the own languages and motivate them. But once a group of men had entered the barricade, the milling crowd of *sadhus* and *kar-sewaks* must have followed and joined them. Once the cordon of Central Reserve Police was breached, there remained no reserve to withhold oneself because of the highly emotionally surcharged atmosphere. This may be partly due to the frustration bred by the injunction artificially kept alive by the High Court by not delivering the judgment in the writ petition. It is strange that the Central Reserve Police, who had taken over the security of the structure and the land inside the barricade, could not or did not prevent this group from entering it.

IV

15. The clinching evidence that there was no conspiracy is furnished by the record. The CBI, which had been entrusted with the investigation of Crime No. 197 of 1992 relating to demolition of the structure, arrested 25 persons (including '*sadhu-sant*' from Balrampur Hospital at Lucknow, where they were being treated for injuries received during demolition of the structure at Ayodhya. In their statements made to the Police, they claimed to have demolished the disputed structure at Sri Rama Janmabhumi on sudden impulse and denied any conspiracy or instigation by any person or accused.

16. They were produced before the Judicial Magistrate CBI, Lucknow (Sri R.D. Paliwal), who remanded them to judicial custody and later, by another order on the same day, released them on bail. The bail was granted on the ground that no offence under sections 295/297/153A were made out and the offence, if any, was only under sections 332, 337, 338 and 427 IPC. The CBI then filed a Criminal Misc. Petition under section 482 Cr.P.C. (registered as Cr. Misc. Case No. 30 of 1993) before the Lucknow Bench of the High Court against these 25 persons released on bail. It prayed for 'setting aside of the order dated 05-01-1993 of the Sub-Judicial Magistrate CBI, Lucknow granting bail to the accused opposite parties. It was further prayed that 'the operation of the aforementioned order granting bail to the accused opposite parties be stayed for pendency of the petition'. This application was accompanied by an affidavit of Sri M. Narayanan, Deputy Superintendent of Police CBI/ SIT, the Chief Investigation Officer in Crime No. 197 of 1992, of Police Station Rama Janmabhumi, Ayodhya.

17. After completion of the investigation, the CBI submitted a consolidated report or police charge-sheet (challan), ***State* v. *Bala Saheb Thackrey*** before Sub-Judicial Magistrate, CBI, Lucknow on 05-10-1993. Strange enough it was without making these self-confessed offenders as accused. There was no reference to them.

18. U.P. Police Regulations prescribe the Form (No. 339) for a Police Report under section 173 Cr.P.C., known as Police charge-sheet or *challan*. This form requires the names of persons, who have been arrested, but not challaned to be mentioned in it. Column 2 of the charge-sheet filed by the CBI in the present case is headed as 'Names and addresses of accused persons not sent for trial, whether arrested or not arrested including absconders'. The charge-sheet filed required a mention of the persons arrested in connection with the crime together with reasons why they were not being sent up for trial. They had injuries on their person received during demolition and were self-condemned. The CBI also filed an application under section 482 Cr.P.C. for cancellation of their bail. It was illegal and *mala fide* for the CBI not to send them for trial.

19. Similarly, PW-2 R.P. Tandon, Dy. S.P. (who had earlier investigated Crime No. 197 of 1992), in his statement made to the CBI, informed that he had arrested 27 persons and one Devendra Singh Rawat, Advocate of Bhopal, from the District Hospital, Faizabad. They had injuries on their person received in the incident. They had stated at the time of arrest that: '*They had demolished the symbol of Mughal slavery and got peace now*'. They also pointed out other associates. It is noteworthy that none of these persons boasting of the alleged crime and arrested at the District Hospital, Faizabad due to injuries received in the incident were named as accused or referred to in the police report (challan).

20. The reason is not far to seek. The Police recorded the statements of persons injured in the incident. They admitted to have demolished the structure 'as it was a symbol of Mughal slavery' and 'to have received injuries in that operation'. They further confessed that 'they did it spontaneously without pre-meditation and on spur of the moment without being instigated by anyone'. All these accused arrested from the Hospital at Lucknow or the District Hospital, Faizabad, who had injuries on their person and had admitted to have taken part in the demolition, were not named in the Police charge-sheet of the CBI and were not challaned. This *mala fide* action was resorted to, as they had denied and completely negatived the theory of conspiracy for the incident or to demolish the structure, a brainchild of the CBI. The whole edifice of the police charge-sheet is now based on the alleged conspiracy, which is completely negatived by the events and the record as noted above.

IV

21. Most probably, it was in the beginning of January 1993 that I had occasion to travel from Lucknow to Delhi by the Lucknow Mail. A late reservation found me in the AC-I compartment. The Government official, who had accompanied the Army Officer (my sole companion in the cabin) to the railway station, introduced me as Former Advocate-General and a lawyer appearing in ***Ram Janmabhumi*** case. Those two had spent some hours at the demolition site in Ayodhya. This set the talks rolling as the train steamed out of the platform. I was given to understand that the Army Officer (an Explosive Expert) had gone to Ayodhya, on orders of the Union Government to find evidence, if any, in support of the theory of explosives being used in the demolition. He found none. On my query that how could such a big building, in which the domes had been rebuilt by the British Government in the year 1934, could be dismantled brick by brick and razed to the ground in a matter of a few hours, he gave a revealing answer. He gave me to understand that it might be a job of experts in demolition, but no explosive was used. I thought of ex-militiamen, but suddenly the thought of Central Armed Police struck me with full force.

22. Believe it or not, the 47 FIRs of media-persons were lodged from 8-12-1992 to 11-03-1993 under various sections of snatching and breaking their films and equipment in different incidents at different times and places against unknown *'kar-sewaks'*. It is apparent that these FIRs were lodged pursuant to the announcement of the Central Government to the media that every person, who suffered loss in the incident at Ayodhya, would be compensated.

V

23. Sri K.S. Sudarshan (*Sar-sanghchalak* of the RSS) sometimes after his deposition before the Liberahan Commission chanced to stay for a few hours at Allahabad. Our talks turned to his statement as reported in the newspapers. A very prominent Muslim Congress Leader (close to the then Prime Minister) had personally informed him about the two letters sent by him soon after the incident to the Prime Minister. In the first letter, he intimated (somethings like this):

> "You know I get information of what happens in your kitchen cabinet. Well the structure in Ayodhya is demolished, but now you should not blame or ban the RSS for it. You can blame VHP, if you like."

It was because of reference to RSS that copies of the letters were shown to *Sar-sanghchalakji* in confidence in the private talks.

VI

24. The investigation of the case has been tardy. Shorn of the allegations relating to snatching or taking away of recording equipment and camera of media people, the offence was triable by a Magistrate Ist Class. There was no question of committal to Sessions. There is no evidence in the Police papers of any conspiracy that is of a meeting of two or more minds together to commit a crime, as is necessary for the offence of conspiracy. Instead of the story put forth in their confession to the Police by self-condemned persons arrested from the hospitals confessing to the injuries in the incident, a phoney story of conspiracy has been built up only to rope in some leaders. The statements of those arrested, who were without any reason not challaned or illegally not shown in the Police charge-sheet destroyed the whole theory of the conspiracy.

CHAPTER 5

Cry Ayodhya, Cry

1. Cry Ayodhya! Who called you a city of peace, where no war ever held the people to ransom? How you have been converted into a city of turmoil? For Ayodhya did become such a centre all over the State of Uttar Pradesh in the second week of November, 2003, when some organisations had chalked a programme for visiting Ayodhya for *'darshan'* and 'puja' of the 'Sri Ram Lala', the Deity there at Sri Ram Janmabhoomi.

2. The previous history is well-known. Dispute having arisen as regards user of the structure at Sri Ram Janmabhoomi, Sub-Divisional Magistrate attached it. He appointed a receiver to look after the *'sewa-puja'* of the deity. The receiver submitted an estimate of expenses for it, which was approved by the court. Soon thereafter, two suits came to be filed for injunction by two worshippers; the first being O.S. No. 2 of 1950 in the Court of the Civil Judge, Faizabad. The court granted a temporary injunction. It was slightly modified on 19-01-1950, "To restrain the authorities (defendants) from removing the idols in question from the site in dispute and interfering with the *'puja'* etc. as at present carried out". In appeal a Division Bench of the High Court confirmed this interim order.

3. Even during the hysteria created after demolition of the structure and consequent executive action, the judiciary did not loose its poise and balance. A Division Bench of the High Court by its judgment ***Vishwa Hindu Adhivakta Sangh* v. *Union of India*, (1993) 1 UPLBEC 501, dated 1-1-1993,** issued a *mandamus* commanding the authorities to allow the petitioners and Hindus and devotees to have *'darshan'* in a meaningful manner at Sri Ram Janmabhoomi at Ayodhya from such a distance, which may not be disproportionate and too for off with reference to devotees and pilgrims view and the vision from outside, but taking note of security of the idol as well as the surrounding circumstances prevailing. Further directions were issued relating to performance of 'puja' and safety of 'pujaris' and idols from vagaries and agony of the weather.

4. This order became embodied in the maintenance of *'status quo'* (as it stood on 7-1-1993) under section 7(2), when the 'Acquisition of Certain Area at Ayodhya Ordinance, 1993' (subsequently Central Act No. 33 of 1993), was promulgated.

5. When the programme for visiting Ayodhya for *'puja'* and 'darshan' at Sri Ram Janmabhoomi was announced by Vishwa Hindu Parishad, an application was moved in O.O.S. No. 4 of 1989, ***Sunni Central Board of Waqfs* v. *Gopal Singh Visharad*** pending under extraordinary jurisdiction of Lucknow Bench of the Allahabad High Court. (It was registered as Civil Misc. Application No. 100(O) of 2003. The prayer was for an order directing Sri Ashok Singhal (not a party in the suit), the State of Uttar Pradesh and District Magistrate, Faizabad "not to hold or permit to hold the declared march to Ayodhya or any public rally there on 17-10-2003 and not to disturb the *status quo* of the disputed site and secondly or restrain them issuing any statement to the press or to the electronic media in the context of Archeological Survey of India report and from propagating amongst the masses that Archeological Survey of India report was in favour of existence of a temple beneath the disputed land".

6. The court by its order dated 10-10-2003 directed maintenance of the *status quo* at the site in dispute. It further expressed the hope "that the State Government and district administration as also the authorized person (under Central Act No. 33 of 1993) will pass necessary orders to regulate the behaviour of the crowd and not allow any congregation on or around the disputed site, and further they shall not permit any religious activity of any kind by any one. However, extraordinary precaution may be pressed into service to see that usual *'puja'* and *'darshan'* is not disturbed."

7. It may be mentioned that the disputed site relating to which this order was passed consisted of the land beneath the old structure, its inner and outer courtyards only.

8. In pursuance of the programme, people from distant parts of India came by rail and road for *'puja'* and *'darshan'* of Sri Ram Lala at Ayodhya. All these persons were checked at the entry points in the State of Uttar Pradesh and proceeding to Ayodhya under sections 107/117 Cr.P. C. Such proceedings take place before an Executive Magistrate requiring the person to furnish security for keeping the peace or for maintaining good behaviour.

9. The Judicial Magistrate then passed a composite order purporting to be under section 107 of the Cr.P.C. authorising detention in jail without drawing the regular proceedings.

10. The only fact alleged in the police report was that these persons were going on the road shouting slogans, thus infringing the order under section 144 Cr.P.C., a thing palpably false. True, an Executive Magistrate can take action where he receives information that there is a person within his jurisdiction, who is likely to commit a breach of the peace or disturb the public tranquility or do any wrongful act beyond his jurisdiction. There was no such information in respect of the passengers going by rail with proper tickets. Moreover, a single *omnibus* order for detention in jail was passed in respect of the persons, whose list was yet to be prepared in the improvised jails.

11. It is inconceivable what happened when proceedings relating to two of these incidents were taken in the High Court at Allahabad and Lucknow. Thirty-three persons had come from Dharwad and some other districts of Karnataka on 13-10-2003. They had proper railway tickets for Ayodhya. They had already boarded the train at Lucknow Junction. The train was checked and all those persons going to Ayodhya among several others were arrested without being informed the ground or offence or the reason for it. Some of them were manhandled, or beaten up. There were teachers, students, businessmen and professionals and law abiding and peaceful citizens. Their only fault was that they wanted to pray at the feet of Sri Ram Lala at his birthplace at Ayodhya. They (the men, women and children all) were taken into custody and herded to Mandi Samiti, which was declared to be a provisional jail along with nearly 250 or 300 others. They were not provided even with water to drink or food or other basic necessities. In their petition under article 226 of the Constitution protesting against the detention, they referred to the order of the Bench trying Sri Ram Janmabhoomi/Babri Masjid suits referred to above. They challenged their arrest and detention by Writ Petition No. 594 of 2003, ***Preep Pattanshelly Hebbulli Agasi* v. *State of Uttar Pradesh.***

12. They also referred to Writ Petition No. 10736 of 1999, ***R.S. Chauhan* v. *State of Uttar Pradesh,*** in which the High Court had directed that the opposite parties shall not arrest the petitioners merely for the reason that they were proceeding to Ayodhya for undertaking *'parikrama'* or religious rites, unless there was violation of any law on their part.

13. The petition also referred to the statement of the Prime Minister "that the function organised by Vishwa Hindu Parishad would be peaceful and the statement of Vishwa Hindu Parishad should be believed" (*vide* Rashtriya Sahara dated 13-10-2003). Photostat copies of various orders and news-items were filed.

14. The writ petition alleged gross violation of law and inhuman conduct of the authorities, who had detained these persons in the Mandi Samiti without providing food or water contrary to the provisions of the Jail Manual and ordinary human conduct. It was further alleged in the petition that the petitioners had not been produced before any Magistrate and their detention was illegal and unconstitutional. It was categorically stated that the petitioners were law-abiding citizens and were not a threat to public order, peace or tranquility and they had been arrested, while going to Ayodhya for pilgrimage.

15. The parameters relating to the orders under section 144 Cr.P.C. or section 151 IPC have been laid down by the Supreme Court in no unmistakable terms. The Supreme Court in the case of ***Gulam Abbas* v. *State of Uttar Pradesh,* AIR 1981 SC 198: 1981 Cr LJ 1835: (1982) 1 SCR 1077** discussed the scope and ambit of section 144 Cr.P.C. In that case it was asserted that "the exercise of the power under section 144 Cr.P.C. has invariably been perverse and in utter disregard of the lawful exercise of legal rights of the Shia communities to perform their religious ceremonies and functions. And instead of being in aid of lawful exercise, it is in favour of those, who unlawfully and illegally interfere with such lawful exercise under the facile ground of prohibition of imminent danger to peace and tranquility of locality".

16. The court by way of providing the local authorities requisite guidelines in that respect discussed the whole matter threadbare. They said, "any exercise of his power under section 144 Cr.P.C., the Magistrate must have (regard to) rights, and subject of course to the paramount consideration of maintenance of public peace and tranquility, the exercise of power must be in aid of those rights and against those, who interfere with the lawful exercise thereof. In other words, the Magistrate's action should be directed against the wrongdoer rather than the wronged.

17. "Furthermore, it would not be proper exercise of discretion on the part of Executive Magistrate to interfere with the lawful exercise of the right by a party on a consideration that those who threaten to interfere constitute a large majority and it would be more convenient for the administration to impose restrictions, which would effect only a minor section of the community rather than prevent a larger section more vociferous and militant".

18. The Supreme Court quoted with approval the observations in ***Sundaram Chetti* v. *The Queen,* ILR 6 Mad 203: 2 Weir 77 (FB).** "Where rights are threatened, the person entitled to them should receive the fullest protection the law affords them and the circumstances admit of. It needs no arguments to prove that the authority of the Magistrate should be exerted in defense of rights rather than any suppression, in the repression of illegal rather than any interference with lawful acts. If the Magistrate is satisfied that the exercise of a right is likely to create a riot, he can hardly be ignorant of the persons from whom disturbance is to be apprehended and it is his duty to take from them security to keep the peace".

19. In the case of ***Madhu Limaye* v. *State of Bihar*, AIR 1971 SC 2486: (1971) 2 SCR 711: (1971) Cr LJ 1721,** the Supreme Court expressed the view that 'the keynote of the power in section 144 Cr.P.C. is to free the society from menace of serious disturbances of a grave character and section is directed against those, who attempt to prevent the exercise of legal rights by others or imperil public safety'.

20. In the present case, there was no other party and there was absolutely no question of any imminent danger to public peace and tranquility merely because a section chose to go on a pilgrimage on a particular occasion has no conceivable connection to public peace and tranquility.

21. Absolutely no facts were alleged and recorded what was the danger and how did the Executive Magistrates of various districts of Uttar Pradesh take into their head that there was imminent danger of public peace and tranquility and that it could not be prevented otherwise than by arresting people going on the pilgrimage to Ayodhya. They could not act as a thought-police of fiction.

22. It passes one's comprehension as to how could any apprehension arise in the circumstances of the case. No facts, no reports regarding it had been alleged in the public or at the time of arrest or during detention. Nor were persons detained ever told as to what the apprehension was and how did it arise.

23. The story of apprehension to public peace and tranquility was apparently a figment of imagination. The question was whether such high-handed action could be justified on the anvil of article 19(5) of the Constitution 'as a reasonable restriction in the interest of the general public', on the right guaranteed by the Constitution under clause (d) of article 19(1).

24. The requirements to be followed in all cases of arrest or detention and deprivation of personal liberty by the Police have been laid down in article 22(1) read with the provisions of the Code of Criminal Procedure. They have been elaborated by decisions of the High Courts and the Supreme Court from time to time, the latest being ***D.K. Basu* v. *State of West Bengal*, (1997) 1 SCC 416: AIR 1997 SC 610: 1997 AIR SCW 233.**

25. It was alleged in the writ petition that these provisions of law were only observed in their breach.

26. Another writ petition was filed at Allahabad being Writ Petition No. 6348 of 2003, ***Manoj Sahu* v. *State of Uttar Pradesh*.** Both these writ petitions raised questions relating to personal liberty of the people, their illegal arrest and detention. These were the questions calling for judicial decision.

27. The Lucknow Bench (Hon'ble Markandey Katju and another JJ) by their order dated 15-10-2003 dismissed the writ petition at the threshold. The judgment reads like an apology of a judicial pronouncement. The court excused itself by observing, "The modern trend points to judicial restraint in administrative acts. The court does not have the expertise to correct the administrative decisions... . If a review of the administrative decision is permitted, it will be substituting its own decision without necessary expertise, which itself may be fallible. "It must be remembered that certain matters which by their very nature are such as better be left to the experts in the field instead of courts themselves seeking to substitute their own views and perceptions. In the present case this court should not interfere in a matter, which relates to the administration, which is in the best position to know about the law and order situation... . Judicial restraint tends to protect the Independence of the judiciary when courts encroach on the legislature or executive feels almost inevitably (that) voters, legislators and other elected officers will conclude that the activities of judges should be closely monitored.

28. "If judges act like legislators or administrators, it follows that judges should be elected like legislators or selected like members of the executive. This is counter-protective. The touchstone of an independent judiciary has been its removal from the political or administrative process. Even if this removal has sometimes been less than complete, it is an ideal worthy of support and one that has valuable effects".

29. What reason or sermonizing to the judiciary itself? It is abdication of judicial functions. It sets at naught and condemns all the decisions of the Supreme Court and the High Courts relating to legality of arrest and detention and deprivation of personal liberty at the hands of the executive. It is a whiff of dark period of judicial inaction during emergency coming back.

30. In the decision in Civil Misc. Writ Petition No. 6348 of 2003, ***Manoj Sahu* v. *State of Uttar Pradesh*** at Allahabad, gave certain directions to the authorities for ameliorating the conditions in which the petitioners were detained. It was in the nature of an interim order. But curiously the writ petition was 'disposed of finally' with it.

31. It fell short of deciding legal questions raised, dismissing them at the admission stage without requiring the authorities to show cause or file any counter-affidavit. The Lucknow Bench shut its eyes to the inhuman conditions alleged in the writ petition.

32. The decision of the Lucknow Bench reminds me of the case of ***Sheela Barse* v. *Union of India*, 1986 Cr LJ 1736: AIR 1986 SC 1773: 1986 (30) DLT 350.** The petition was for release of juveniles from illegal detention in jails, they were kept there along with hardened criminals.

33. She had pointed out that "a majority of children had been in prison for three years or more despite the Children's Acts in most States and Union Territories clearly forbidding the authorities to imprison juveniles". This called for a quick judicial decision.

34. The Supreme Court, however, dilly-dallied and again and again gave time to the States to come forward with certain particulars. Ultimately, her patience was exhausted and she filed an application for withdrawing the petition. The Supreme Court said "........ Unduly harsh and coercive measures against the State authorities might themselves become counter-productive. In the matter of affirmative action the willing co-operation of the authorities must, as far as possible, be explored".

35. Seervai, in his famous book *'Constitution of India'*, remarked, "To carry on the persuasion for 20 months is an abdication of Supreme Court's judicial power and is disregard of the judicial oath to uphold the Constitution and the law.

36. In the end he said, "In my submission the judgments delivered... (their particulars were given) must make layman lawyers and judges bow their head in shame".

37. The writ petitions relating to the legality to arrest and detention of persons going for pilgrimage to Ayodhya en-route at various entry points in Uttar Pradesh called for a judicial pronouncement.

38. To dismiss the writ petition on executive considerations without calling on the persons responsible for showing cause why they arrested and detained the petitioners makes the High Court dysfunctional.

39. I have yet to see any other case where a petition alleging illegal detention has been thrown out *in limine* without requiring the detaining authority to show cause and to decide the legality of detention under the extraordinary excuse advanced.

40. Lord Denning was once asked why he did not read daily newspapers. His reply was that he 'did not want the newspaper to try the case before him'.

41. It seems this salutary practice was lost. A section of the English media, hostile for petty political gains, and the phantom genie it un-bottled has won and justice lost.

42. All the more surprising is that this happened at the hands of the professed "sentinel on the *qui vive*", to whom the Constitution entrusted its most valuable gift, the liberty of person. Were persons going for *'darshan'* and *'puja'* to Ayodhya second-rate citizens?

CHAPTER 6

The Kashmir Imbroglio

I

1. A story is told of an artist, who was painting a picture of Lord Ganesh. As ill luck had it, the trunk got stuck at the back, as a caricature of a tail. And *lo*, the picture of a monkey stared at his face. This is the story of Kashmir under the Nehru dispensation of wrong premises and perverted politics.

2. Said Jagmohan, former Governor of Jammu and Kashmir (J&K in short), "Had we followed Dr. Shyama Prasad Mookerji, there would have been no Kashmir problem". The slogan, '*ek vidhan, ek nishan, ek pradhan*', which was the reason of his martyrdom, is still the only rational basis on which any lasting edifice can be built. The Government of India is bogged into a quagmire and legal quibbling.

3. The story of treachery, which gave way to Pakistan fighting a proxy war in Kashmir, is too well-known. What is not so well-known is the role of saviour played by Sardar Patel in the accession of J&K to the Indian Union. It was Sardar Patel's achievement, not only thwarting the British scheme of Balkanisation of the country, but also securing the accession of J&K to India, in spite of odds, the conditions and vacillations of Pt. Nehru, and the snares woven by the British.

4. After the announcement of June 3, 1947, the Ruler of J&K was in a dilemma. All means of communication of the State of J&K including postal and telegraph services lay through the territory, which was to be included in Pakistan.

There was no independent link with the rest of India. Sri V.P. Menon tells us (*vide* the Story of Integration of the Indian States) of the efforts of Lord Mountbatten, who flew to Kashmir for four days in the third week of June in a bid to secure the accession of Kashmir to Pakistan. The Maharaja of Kashmir had to invent an excuse that he was ill and confined to bed; he begged to be excused for the last meeting on the fourth day. In the midst of all forces of the British thus aligned in one way, with the vicious propaganda of Muslim League organising riots all round the country, and engineering revolt of Muslim soldiers in Maharaja's armed forces, Pakistan mounted pressure tactics.

5. Sardar Patel was aware of what was brewing. In this dire hour of need of India, he wanted some leader of all India stature, in whom both he and the Maharaja could repose absolute confidence in the delicate mission he was entrusting. The choice fell on Sri M.S. Golwalkar (Sri Guruji to many). He was flown to Srinagar in a State plane on 17-10-1947. On return (on the 19th), Sri Golwalkar conveyed to Sardar Patel the glad news of the readiness of the Maharaja to accede to India (The full story is told in 'The Tragic Story of Partition' by H.V. Sheshadri)

6. In the meantime, the State needed a new Prime Minister to cope with the situation. The choice fell on an illustrious lawyer and Judge of the Lahore High Court, Sri Mehar Chand Mahajan (later Chief Justice of India). Sardar Patel has full faith in him and his ability. The biographer of Mahajan tells us, "Sardar Patel not only encouraged Justice Mahajan but practically ordered him to accept the prime ministership and proceed to Srinagar. He was granted eight months' leave and permission to take up service in the State of J&K, 'in the larger interests of India.' (*vide* 'Chief Justice Mehar Chand Mahajan' by Dr. Vidya Dhar Mahajan) Mahajan took over as Prime Minister of J&K on 15-10-1947.

7. The attack of Pakistan in the guise of tribesmen began on 23-10-1947. The story is recounted in 'The Tragic Story of Partition' (*supra*). It tells us how the snow was cleared at the Srinagar airport for Indian planes to land and of the matching of courage and military skill of the Indian Jawans (soldiers) and the heroic assistance of the volunteers of the Rashtriya Swayam-Sewak Sangh. The rest is current history.

II

8. Then Pt. Nehru intervened and took over from Sardar Patel the affairs of the State of J&K. His friend Sheikh Abdulla was installed at his insistence as 'Prime Minister' of J&K. Sheikh Abdulla signed the agreement for complete merger of the State as other Indian States and flew to Srinagar. He however returned by the next flight with two Government Secretaries and new demands. Result was not only a special status, but also a guarantee of a separate constitution by another constituent assembly to be convened in future for the State of J&K.

9. The representatives of that State took part in the deliberations of the Constituent Assembly of the country. The propriety and legality of procedure of the Constituent Assembly of India abdicating its task, *qua* the State of J&K, to another assembly in future is open to doubt. It amounted to fraud on the country. The whim of Pt. Nehru resulted in the anomaly as article 370.

III

10. The later events created the catastrophe of hounding the Hindus (the Kashmiri Pandits) out of the Kashmir valley. They became refugees in their own country. There is an effort, by hook or crook, to change the demographic complexion of the Jammu and Laddakh regions and settle them by Kashmiri Muslims.

11. Jammu and Laddakh are a tragic tale of intense discrimination and apathy on the part of the State Government and deprivation of civic rights to a substantial part of population. Further the story of step-motherly treatment those regions is writ large. It is worked with a fine comb in every sphere of life, so that Jammu and Laddakh get a pittance, when compared to the share Kashmir gets out of national income or wealth. The list of the deprivations of the residents of Jammu and Laddakh (both Hindus and Muslims) is endless and encompasses every sphere of life. Let us look at the statistics till the year 2002, when this article was first penned, available from official sources.

12. The respective areas and population of the three regions are Jammu 26,293 Sq. Kms. with 24,61,906 voters in the Parliamentary elections, Kashmir 15,853 Sq. Kms. with 24,10,220 electors, and Laddakh 59,241 Sq. Kms. with 63,597 electors. Yet, Jammu elects 2 members to the Parliament, and 37 to the State Assembly, Kashmir 3 and 46, and Laddakh 1 (being a separate ethnic area) to the Parliament and 4 to the State Assembly. In the administrative set up Jammu has 4 offices of the commissioners/secretaries rank, while Kashmir 31. Percentage of the employees in the Civil Secretariat from Jammu region is 10% while from Kashmir 90%. The headquarter of Central Government, offices and all the 13 State Corps are located in Kashmir with 100% Kashmiri employees. The total revenues from Jammu region are 70%, while from Kashmir 30%. Yet the figures are reversed when it comes to expenditure, namely only 30% (including Central assistance) is spent in Jammu; while 70% on Kashmir. This is more marked in the spending of Central funds; the figures are 10% for Jammu and 90% for Kashmir. The figures for special funds from the Prime Minister in 1986 were only 8% for Jammu but 92% for Kashmir.

13. Similarly, for amenities for tourists. More than 50 lac tourists per year come to Jammu. The State spends a bare 10% on them. On the other hand, tourist inflow in Kashmir is less than 2 lacs while it allocates 90% of Government expenditure on them. The electric power generation in Jammu region is 350 Mega Watt, with nil in Kashmir region. Yet, the share of power given to Jammu region is only 22 Mega Watt as against 328 Mega Watt in Kashmir. Government expenditure on power generated is 10 crores for Jammu region, while for Kashmir, it is 490 crores.

14. Similar situation exists in the educational field. Of academic institutions: 65% are located in Jammu, but the region gets only 30% of State expenditure on them. On the other hand, 35% of the academic institutions in

Kashmir get 70% of the total expenditure. In professional courses, there are a good number of Kashmiri students in Jammu institutions (by official orders), while students from Jammu form a microscopic fraction in Kashmir institutions. Institutions like Ayurvedic College or Agricultural College located in Jammu have been closed down. The Veterinary College, Dental College, Artificial Limb Centre and Physical Training College proposed for Jammu have been set up in Kashmir. The current Government has reduced the share of Jammu students in professional institutions from 45% to 20%. The number of unemployed educated youth as on August 1989 is put for Jammu at 42,000 while for Kashmir at 26,784. Contrast this with employment provided by the State since 1996. The figures are 15,000 for Jammu region, while 1,40,000 for Kashmir.

15. The imbalance, in the seats allotted to different regions in the Vidhan Sabha resulted in there being no Chief Minister from Jammu region. The ministers from that region are in a minority with unimportant portfolios. The refugees from 'Pak-Occupied Kashmir' in 1947 were not allowed to settle in Kashmir, but were rehabilitated in Jammu. In the same year 3-4 lacs of refugees from across the international border in Jammu region were not given the status of a State subject. They are disenfranchised for Assembly elections, denied government jobs, education, right to property. They are not citizens of J and K State.

16. The story is unending. The Gajendragadkar, Sikri and Wazir Commissions have come and gone; yet the grievances of the people of Jammu and Laddakh remain. The State Government failed (in spite of voluminous Central aid) to implement these recommendations. Even the utterances of Ex-Governors of J and K characterising the Kashmiri leaders of the time to be in league with the separatists have been cries in wilderness.

17. A lawyer friend of mine, when I was once in Jammu, told me,

"Our relations, refugees from parts of Punjab and Kashmir, who have been here since they were chased out of their hearths and homes in 1946 and 1947, still after more than 50 years of being domiciled in the State have no right to vote in the State Assembly; although as citizens of India they vote in the Parliamentary election. These refugees lost almost everything they had, except their faith in God and their country. They, single-handed built up the economy here, yet are not citizens of this blessed State. They cannot get employment here in the State, and cannot buy any landed property. If a Kashmiri woman marries outside the State (or a refugee domiciled here), she looses her citizenship of the State; but a refugee girl marrying a Kashmiri does not get it".

In a voice choked with emotion he almost wailed,

"Cry my beloved country of equality of status and opportunity of justice and liberty of faith and worship, the land of fraternity assuring dignity to every individual, the land of fundamental rights ensuring to its citizens fair play and a decent life (words of Preamble of both constitutions). Cry for your unfortunate and helpless children, the children born or domiciled in this alleged heaven on earth. Cry mother, cry for them."

IV

18. Irked by horrendous hostile discrimination, the Vishwa Hindu Parishad and the Rashtriya Swayam-Sewak Sangh (RSS), contrary to their earlier stand, passed resolutions for reorganisation of the State of J&K into 3 distinct units (the fourth being 'Pak-Occupied Kashmir'). The reason is writ large in the blatant discrimination by the State Government, defying all logic and reason, against the people of Jammu and Laddakh. Even the Muslims of these regions have joined hands with others in raising the demand. The agitation has been simmering for years, to which recent laws, policies and actions of the State Government, have added fuel to fire.

THE KASHMIR IMBROGLIO—PART II

V

19. All this calls for examination of the problem in depth and its remedy. A strange web of legalism is now woven around article 370 of the Constitution: 'It is the only tie between the State of J&K with the rest of India and once it is snapped the bond will be broken.' This is incorrect. The instrument of accession of the Maharaja of J&K (Sri Hari Singh) was in the same terms as executed by other rulers. The Dominion of India thus acquired jurisdiction over that State with respect to defence, external affairs and communications. Article 1(3) speaks of the territory of India as comprising the territories of the States (including Part B State of J&K). Article 370(1) clause (c) itself speaks that article 1 of the Constitution applies to that State. Section 3 of the Constitution of the State of J&K, states that *"The State of J&K is and shall be an integral part of the Union of India"*. Thus the State of J&K (including 'Pak-Occupied Kashmir') is a part of India. Moreover, section 3 (*supra*) declaring the State of J & K an integral part of India cannot be amended.

20. True, under article 370(1), its clauses and provisos attached to it, the power of the Parliament to legislate in respect of subjects in the Union List and the Concurrent List (which do not relate to the subjects corresponding to those specified in the Instrument of Accession) cannot be exercised in the absence of the concurrence of the State Government, *vide* the second proviso. But the real teeth of discrimination lie in article 35A introduced under 'The Constitution (Application to Jammu and Kashmir) Order, 1954' promulgated by the President (hereinafter referred to as the Presidential Order). It failed to confer the fundamental right of equality before law to all the people born and bred up in the State of J&K and to the citizens of India.

21. 'Permanent Residents defined in section 6 of the Constitution of Jammu and Kashmir as 'a State subject of class I or class II as defined in the notification of the Maharaja dated 20-04-1927'. Therein 'State Subject class I' is defined as one born and residing within the State before the close of Samvat, 1942 (March, 1885 AD) and has since permanently resided there. 'Class II' comprises those (other than belonging to class I) who had settled within the State before the close of Samvat, 1968 (March, 1911 AD) and have since permanently resided and acquired immovable property within the State.

Add to them, those who acquired immovable property in the State of Jammu and Kashmir in pursuance of an *izazatnama* granted by the State and were ordinarily resident in the State for less than 10 years prior to the commencement of the Presidential Orders dated 14-05-1954. What a sop?

22. This obviously makes the State of Jammu and Kashmir more or less a closed house. We may take it that this definition includes the issues of the 'State Subjects'. Practically, it hands over the State to a few, without taking into account the sea-change in the country. In particular it fails to consider the holocaust, the partition and the birth of two countries India and Pakistan, the influx of refugees, dawn of democracy in India based on equality and adult franchise and the whole history of a hundred years. The constitution of J&K makes a mockery of ideas of a free democracy and notions of International law regarding citizenship. It is a ploy to concentrate power of the State into a few hands. It reduces a substantial section of the Indian people in Kashmir to the status of second rate, nay non-citizens. When will the Supreme Court take cognizance of this fraud and declare it unconstitutional.

23. Article 35A added by the Presidential Order enables abrogation of fundamental rights of the people (other than those artificially defined as 'permanent residents') regarding (i) employment in the State of J&K, (ii) acquisition of immovable property there, (iii) settlement in J&K and (iv) right to scholarship and such other forms of aid the State may provide. Even the highly artificial definition of a 'permanent resident' (*otiose* and which in certain context defies all logic) cannot be changed. The provisions thus give all the aforesaid rights to persons called 'permanent residents' only, but not to persons ordinarily living or domiciled in the State of J&K or born there, unless born to a 'State subject of class I or II'.

24. The hostility of the provisions is apparent. The artificially defined 'permanent residents' of Kashmir get all fundamental rights throughout the length and breadth of the country; while others, even though they may be living in the State of J&K since before the partition of India, their children or citizens of the rest of India get no rights in the State. This is so, even if the person was born and bred up in J&K. He cannot get government service, admission in colleges enabling him to pursue the learned professions, and he has no right to vote in the Legislative Assembly. He cannot purchase property in the State. The so-called 'permanent residents' of J&K on the other hand get all these rights in the rest of India. If a woman, a 'permanent resident' of J&K marries a person not a 'permanent resident' though domiciled in J&K, she looses all rights; probably her right to landed property there also. The list of such hostile rules is endless. It presents a bedlam, which defies the sense of justice and reason.

25. The remedy obviously lies in full integration of the State, placing it at par with other States. This cannot be done through orders passed under article 370(1), without the concurrence of J&K Government. This results in a stalemate. In the meantime, the State of J&K has passed a law enabling former residents, now citizens of Pakistan or Pak-occupied Kashmir to become a 'permanent resident' of the State of J&K. In the result, an alien will become a citizen of India entitled to all the rights in India including fundamental rights. This poses grave threat to integrity and sovereignty of India.

26. A person living in J&K since before partition of India and born there has a right to vote for election to the Parliament but has no right to vote in the elections for State Assembly or Local Self-Government. He or his children are denied franchise in the Sate. Under the constitution of J&K, they are not citizens of that State. Neither he, nor any other citizen of India (other than the alleged 'permanent resident'), can have rights in J&K, although artificially defined 'permanent residents' have all the rights guaranteed under the Constitution, in the rest of India. This clearly violates article 14, it does not apply, except in respect of 'permanent residents' of J&K by virtue of added article 35A. Even the word 'secular' inserted in the Preamble to the Constitution by the 42nd Amendment does not apply to the State of J&K.

VI

27. The right to equality is the basis of an egalitarian society and basic feature of the Constitution. Even as far back as 1943, we had the Reciprocity Act, which enabled the Central Government to impose reciprocal disabilities on persons domiciled in British possessions. In independent India, the Presidential Order has thrown to winds this basic feature of equality. Article 35A enabled the State of J&K to be isolated from the rest of the country. Such an amendment or modification in the shape of article 35A is *ultra vires*, on the dictum laid down in ***Keshwanand Bharati's* case, AIR 1973 SC 1461: (1973) 4 SCC 225** and the decision that follow it. The Parliament could not amend the Constitution in such a fashion, abrogating fundamental right of equality under article 368.

28. Can the power of the President to modify the Constitution in application to J&K contravene the basic feature of the Constitution? This will have to be answered on fundamental principles of constitutional and international law. Earlier it was thought that the judicial review did not extend to certain laws and orders passed under the Constitutional powers. But now the Supreme Court has ruled in ***I.R. Coelho* v. *State of Tamil Nadu*, (2007) 2 SCC 1: AIR 2007 SC 861: 2007 AIR SCW 611** that the judicial review is an integral part of the basic structure of the Constitution and cannot be taken away. Can there be citizens of India, who are not citizens or second rate citizens in the State of J&K and thus not entitled to ordinary civic rights, although State subjects enjoy full citizenship rights in the rest of the country?

VII

29. There has been a persistent demand for repeal of article 370. The Constitution can only be amended under article 368, which does not apply to the State of J&K. Article 370 is said to be the sole repository of all the powers exercisable under the Constitution in relation to the State of J&K and article 368 of the Constitution cannot be invoked to amend or rescind it. What then is the remedy? The answer lies in article 370 itself. The Constitution cannot be applied except under the power granted by this article. It contains, by itself, its death knell. Sub-article (3) of article 370 provides that:

> *"(3) Notwithstanding anything in the foregoing provisions of this article, the President may, by public notification, declare that this article shall cease to be operative,......."*

30. The article ceases to be operative on a public notification to that effect by the President under sub-article (3). Nothing (except the Proviso to this sub-article) stops the President from declaring that article 370 shall cease to be operative as far as Jammu and Laddakh regions (and 'Pak-Occupied Kashmir') are concerned. As soon as article 370 ceases to operate, these regions, as integral part of the Union of India, become wholly governed by the Constitution. However, to this sub-article (3) is added a proviso:

> *"Provided that the recommendation of the Constituent Assembly of the State of J&K referred to in clause (2) shall be necessary before the President issues such a notification."*

31. This proviso is co-extensive with sub-article (2). It is apparent that the Constitution envisaged a situation, when recourse could be had to the Constituent Assembly of the State of J&K. In case the subject-matter of the lists in the Seventh Schedule were to be changed under clause (2) before the Constituent Assembly was convened or it continued in deliberations, the concurrence required was that of the Constituent Assembly, in place of the Government.

32. The Constituent Assembly of the State of J&K has been wound-up. It has finished its task and ceased to exist. Surely, when it is no longer in existence, the proviso to sub-article (3) cannot apply. The law does not contemplate compliance of something impossible. Under the well-known rule of interpretation of statutes, it must be held that the proviso to sub-article (3) applied only during the existence of the Constituent Assembly and cannot apply thereafter. Sub-article (3) was inserted in article 370 to provide a means for withering away of that article; as article 368 (relating to amendment of the Constitution) did not apply to the State of J&K. The object will be wholly frustrated if concurrence of an Assembly, not in existence, is insisted. The maxim of law applicable is *"lex non cogit ad impossible"* (the law does not compel a man to do that which he cannot possibly perform).

33. It will be noticed that this proviso to sub-article (3) does not refer to the Government of the State of J&K. It does not enter into the picture for exercise of powers by the President under that sub-article. Once it is clear that the concurrence of the Constituent Assembly becomes impossible because it has ceased to exist, this clause no longer applies under the law. Reading the two sister provisions together, the requirement of concurrence of the Constituent Assembly of the State of J&K was confined to its life-time.

34. This is, however, not the journey's end. The Presidential Order had also added a proviso to article 3, which empowered the Parliament, *inter alia,* to form new States by separation of territory from any State or change the area and extent and name of any State. The Presidential Order of 1954 has modified this article. The amendment provides that no Bill providing for alteration of its name or change in area shall be introduced in the Parliament without consent of Legislature of the State of J&K. As soon as article 370 ceases to exist for any part, this Presidential Order stands abrogated for that region and the Constitution in its original form begins to apply.

35. But article 3 of the Constitution itself contains a proviso. This Proviso requires that a Bill for the purpose of altering the area or name of the State shall not be introduced except on the recommendation of the President, and that too after the Legislature of the State has been afforded an opportunity to express its views on the proposal. It is noteworthy that the 'consent' of the Legislature of the State is not required for the recommendation to be made (as under the proviso added by the Presidential Order.

36. The declaration that provisions of article 370 will cease to apply to the Jammu and Laddakh regions will entail automatic division of the State. As a matter of law, the two powers, one under article 370(3) of the Constitution and another under the Proviso to article 3 thereof, are different and for different purposes. They are independent provisions and operate in different fields or levels. It was for this reason that article 3 was applied with amended proviso to the State of J&K. The two powers can be exercised independently of each other. If this is correct, the notification under article 370(3) can be made independently of the Proviso to article 3, although it will have the effect of creation of new States or territories.

37. There is, thus, no hurdle in law in making a declaration under sub-article (3) of article 370 that the article will cease to be operative to the Jammu and Laddakh regions (and for that matter in 'Pak-occupied Kashmir'). The decision about the valley can await the future. The Jammu and Laddakh regions can be put simultaneously under the Central rule, until future democratic set-up is determined for them. In the alternative, provision can be made by Ordinance, under article 123 of the Constitution, constituting advisory council consisting of all members in the Legislative Assembly of the State of J&K from respective regions to aid the Administrator appointed for them. The 'Pak-Occupied Kashmir' can await its liberation but will be freed from the shackles of article 370. The Kashmir valley will continue to be governed by article 370.

38. The nightmare of the people of Jammu and Laddakh will be over; mutual struggle ended. These regions will cease to be a fiefdom of the people of Kashmir valley and under the threat of a demographic change (as happened in the valley). The terrorism in the fair land will be contained and the evil designs of Pakistan frustrated. Moreover, the heavenly concept of equality before the law for all citizens, banished from the State, will dawn heralding a new era.

VIII

39. The earlier view that Parliament is supreme and the Courts cannot interfere with its exercise of power under article 368 to amend the Constitution, is no longer tenable. It is now well-settled and established that the power to amend the Constitution under article 368 does not extend to alter the basic feature of the Constitution. The courts have been saved from a great calamity. *See* Chapter 1 entitled 'Reservation now of any kind is Unconstitutional' paragraph 33.

40. It follows that the basic structure of the Constitution cannot be amended. It follows that the order of the President made under article 370 namely, 'The Constitution (Application to the State of Jammu and Kashmir) Order, 1954', insofar as it abrogated article 14 in its application to that State is also *ultra vires* of the power conferred on the President. No citizen of India can be deprived of a right to vote in the election to the State Assembly and cannot be deprived of the right to equality.

41. It is clear that real independence will down upon all the people of Jammu and Kashmir once it is held that article 35A added by the Order of the President is unconstitutional. The State of Jammu and Kashmir will shed the shackles of article 370.

APPENDICES

I. Article 35A added by 'The Constitution (Application to Jammu and Kashmir) Order, 1954'.

"Art. 35A. Notwithstanding anything contained in this Constitution, no existing law in force in the State of Jammu & Kashmir, and no law hereafter enacted by the Legislature of the State—

- **(a)** Defining the classes of persons who are, or shall be, permanent residents of the State of Jammu and Kashmir; or
- **(b)** Conferring on such permanent residents any special rights and privileges, or imposing upon other persons any restrictions, as respects—
  - **(i)** employment under the State Government;
  - **(ii)** acquisition of immovable property in the State;
  - **(iii)** settlement in the State; or
  - **(iv)** right to scholarships and such other forms of aid as the State Government may provide, shall

be void on the ground that it is inconsistent with or takes away or abridges any rights conferred on the other citizens of India by any provisions of this Part".

II. Provisos added to articles 3 and 368 by the aforesaid Presidential Order of 1954):

(A) Proviso added to article 3 of the Constitution relating to "Formation of new States and alteration of areas, boundary or names of existing State (*vide* heading) added by the Constitution (Application to Jammu and Kashmir) Order, 1954, C.O. 48 section 2(2):

"Provided further that no Bill providing for increasing or diminishing the area of the State of Jammu and Kashmir or altering the name or boundary of the State shall be introduced in the Parliament without the consent of the legislature of the State."

(B) Proviso to article 368 of the Constitution of India added by the Constitution (Application to Jammu and Kashmir) Order, 1954.

"Provided further that no such amendment shall have effect in relation to the State of Jammu and Kashmir unless applied by order of the President under clause (1) of article 370."

III. Provisions of Jammu and Kashmir State Constitution: Sections 1, 3, 4, 5 and 147.

1. Short title and commencement.—(1) This Constitution may be called the Constitution of Jammu and Kashmir.

(2) This section and sections 2, 3, 4, 5, 6, 7, 8 and 158 shall come into force at once and the remaining provisions of the Constitution shall come into force on the twenty-sixth day of January, 1957, which day is referred to in this constitution as the commencement of this Constitution.

....

3. Relationship of the State with the Union of India.—The State of Jammu and Kashmir is and shall be an integral part of the Union of India.

4. Territory of the State.—The territory of the State shall comprise all the territories which on the fifteenth day of August, 1947, were under the sovereignty of suzerainty of the Ruler of the State.

5. Extent of Executive and Legislative Power of the State.—The executive and legislative power of the State extends to all matters except those with respect to which Parliament has power to make laws for the State under the Provisions of the Constitution of India.

....

147. Amendment of the Constitution.—An amendment of the Constitution may be initiated only by the introduction of a Bill for the purpose in the Legislative Assembly, and when the Bill is passed in the House by a majority of not less than two-third of the total membership of that House, it shall be presented to the Governor for his assent and upon such assent being given to the Bill, the Constitution shall stand amended in accordance with the terms of the Bill:

Provided that a Bill providing for the abolition of the Legislative Council may be introduced in the Legislative Assembly and passed by it by a majority of the total membership of Assembly and by a majority of not less than two-thirds of the members of the Assembly present and voting:

Provided further that no bill or amendment seeking to make any change in—

(a) this section; or

(b) the provisions of sections 3 and 5; or

(c) the provisions of the Constitution of India as applicable in relation to the State, shall be introduced or moved in either House of the Legislature.

CHAPTER 7

Education and the Law – The Flim-Flam

I.

1. During my primary and secondary education in mid-twenties to mid-thirties my parents subscribed a popular children's monthly magazine called 'Shishu' (child). It carried an invocation and a motto on the title page. 'Arise, arise children of Bharat keep the image of the motherland in your hearts to meditate. You are her only hope, Bharat Mata is looking up to you.' ("उठो, उठो भारत संतान, हृदय धरो माता का ध्यान।। तुम ही पर आशा है सारी, मुख निरखे भारत महतारी।।") There was the invocation and the motto every time the magazine came. My mother asked me to read it loudly. It became the lode-star of our lives.

2. It was the height of repression under the British Rule. This throughout the struggles for independence was one dominant idea in our lives, 'The British Rule must go' throughout our student life. I had read the lives of revolutionaries in my mother's library before the alien government proscribed them. Some day we hoped there would be national education and not one to make us clerks and servants of the British Rule. The feeling permeated into our lives throughout the country.

II

3. During the freedom struggle we had dreams that on achieving independence, we shall have an education programme to weld the nation. During the foreign rule the education, instead of creating a national consciousness, has denationalized us. Our ways were ridiculed. Instead of an urge to find the real meaning of our ancient literature it was sarcastically termed as 'songs of shepherds' (गडरियों के गीत). The calumny heaped on us for every thing which gave rise to national pride, was endless.

4. This policy had continued since the Mugal rule. The British further created zones called Tribal Areas in the name of preserving 'indigenous' (?) culture of that region in which only Christian priests (*'padrie'*) could go to preach, thus alienating them from the national stream of Indian life. The country was forced to forget the Bharat Mata during foreign rule.

5. The depth of feeling can be gauged by a small incident. As a child once I told my father to get for me a bat, as I wanted to play cricket. My father was a sportsman; a reputed player of hockey, football, volleyball and even tennis. To my surprise he said, "Why? Only slaves of the British rule play cricket. Why not play hockey and all other games". During his time as Chairman of education committee of the District Board, Banda, the district achieved the first position in provincial Olympics. He said "You play hockey in which our country became the champion in the Olympics, when United States of America became independent, it banned the game of Cricket". There was a game called 'croquet', they characterized it their national game, and changed its name to 'base-ball'. (It is just like '*gend-danda*, which is played in our villages.) Barnard Shaw, the famous English author, being asked why he did not watch the cricket match replied, "It is a game where two fools run, eleven fools field and a thousand fools watch. I do not want to be one of them". So deep was the feeling and the urge for independence that people burnt British manufactured clothes publicly and boycotted the British goods. We had hopped that India would achieve freedom and the education, which gave vent to this national feeling, would be adopted.

III

6. The subject of education initially was divided into three parts, when the Constitution came into force, *vide* entry 63 to 66 of list I (Union list), entries 11 and 14 of list II (State list), and a part entry 25 of list III (Concurrent List). This was not conducive to national education. By the Constitution (Forty-Second) Amendment Act, 1976 the schedule was amended and a comprehensive entry was adopted in the Concurrent List as entry 25 of list III.

7. In the nineties of the last century I wrote an article 'Aberration in Education Must Go'. It is printed as appendix IV in my book 'Ivory Tower' (published by Universal Book Traders, New Delhi). It *inter-alia*, is as follows:

8. "Even after 46 years of the first taste of independence, we have not shaken what can be called mental slavery. During the long struggle for independence, we had our own ideas of 'nationalism', 'human values' and '*swatantarta*' (our system of self-rule). Slowly, these concepts have been eroded and their place taken by fake editions moulded in western thought by so-called pseudo-secularists. This is most pronounced in the field of education, which has tended to uproot our young men from their national moorings. The soul of India or its culture, the ethos, not only finds no expression in the school curriculum, but in many ways denigrate it".

9. "We go on teaching Dalton's atomic theory, forgetting the first definition of atom ('*parmanu*') and molecule ('*anu*') by Kanad (200 BC) long before the '*samvat*' era. ('Kanad' literally means one who lives by eating particles.) We go on teaching the story of the fallen apple of Newton, oblivious of the 'gravitational law' pronounced in '*Vaisheshik Darshan*'. It said, 'the arrow begins to fall towards the earth when the energy (momentum) imparted by the string of the bow is overcome by the gravitational force of the earth'. We still teach that Gallileo and Copernicus were the first to discover that the earth revolved round the sun, forgetting the sixth stanza of third chapter of '*Yajurved*' (4000 BC) that 'the earth' wearing the green apparel of species and vegetation performs the '*parikrama*' (rounds) of the Sun, giving rise to the seasons.

If we have to talk about Gallileo, let it be told that the *thekedars* of the liberal religion (the Catholics) imprisoned him for life (for 8 years till his death) for representing, contrary to the Bible.

10. "The story of misrepresentation of our science and culture is appalling. The science of Geometry goes by the name of 'Euclid' in Europe. We teach the theorem of Pythogorus (*Peethguru*), forgetting that centuries before him Baudhayan enunciated it in connection with construction of a *'vedi'* (altar). In India, in the beginning of nineteenth century 'arithmetic' was known by the famous book *'Lilawati'*. How many students are told about Lilawati (the widowed daughter of Bhaskaracharya), who first enunciated *'ekikniyam'* in modern form, and envisaged an infinite series having a finite sum. We have forgotten Bhaskaracharya's 'jyan'; ;ज्यां) and 'kojyan' (कोज्या) and remember its corrupted form, 'sine' and 'cosine' in mathematics. We swear by the Darwin's theory of evolution, but have forgotten Patanjali's thesis that 'human life is obtained after going through 84 lakh (8.4 million) forms of species' and that 'nature adopts itself to suit the climes.' We know of about 8 million species today".

11. "But the biggest misrepresentation is in history. We teach the irrational and purposive theory of *'Aryans'* having come from outside, and having vanquished the *'Dravids'*, that these were two different races, setting into motion divisive sentiments, against all logic and evidence of modern research; and still hope that separatism will not rear its head. To top all, we have named the various chapters of our history, the longest in the world, according to tyrannical spells of foreign invaders or despots and call it our history. The country forgot them after vanquishing the Greeks, the Huns and the Kushans. Yet, the victories are hidden or misrepresented. The history teachers have failed to divide the periods of history according to national heroes and glorious achievements of our people of the time in question in science and humanities. It is folly to think that wounds of history are healed by covering them up, and not by learning lessons from them. Actually, the truth is the best healer".

12. "But, in the new wave of 'negationism' (blatant perversion of history) truth is the first casualty. 'Negationism' is a new concept in modern European philosophy, born out of attempted revival of Nazis or *Stalinists* that they were so good, they were not responsible for genocide or crimes against humanity. Similarly speaks their Indian counterpart, 'The Muslim invaders' rule in India was benign, they destroyed the temples not because they hated the culture and wanted to teach the People of India a bitter lesson, but because the temples were rich and they want to get the loot. They wanted to teach the lessons of Akbar the Great, forgetting his 250 women *'harem'* and Meena Bazaar. And recently the decision of a group of Rajasthan bureaucrats is reported, refusing to eulogize the struggle for freedom and the great sacrifice of Rana Pratap in the correct perspective in history textbooks.

13. It must be remembered that 'negationism' (perversion of history by denying the truth as we know it) has been declared to be a crime in certain countries of Europe. In India, what is a crime against the nation receives panegyrics and acclaim of a sect of people, instead of punishment.

14. 'How widespread and deep is the malady can be appreciated by the fact, that, it was reported in the Lucknow papers a month or so ago that a sitting Judge of the Allahabad High Court addressed a public seminar, convened for Sri Ram Bilas Paswan and the convener of the Babri Masjid Action Committee among others. Believe it or not, the Hon'ble Judge is reported to have denounced, in his public speech, the broadcast by Doordarshan of the great epics *'the Ramayan'* and *'the Mahabharat'* as being unconstitutional and illegal, as murdering secularism'. The learned Judge forgot in his zeal that *'the Ramayan'* and *'the Mahabharat'* are great epics and cultural heritage of our motherland and have nothing to do with religion.

15. "For religion has something to do with one's relation to one's God. Goebbelsian propaganda in various forms meets the eye. There, *'Jai Sri Ram'* or *Jai Ramji Ki'* are communal slogans and greetings. The Prophet Mohammed or Jesus Christ started a religion (*'panth'*) and shouting their 'Jai' may be a religious slogan. But, Ram never started or propagated any *'panth'* (religious order), and shouting his *'Jai'* can never be an appeal to religion. The contrary assertions of so-called 'secularists' are invidious discrimination, which hurts the country. We may refer to Justice Bahri, who in his opinion on the ban on Rastriya Swayamsewak Sangh, has called the restoration of Sri Ram Janma Bhumi by itself a 'laudable object' ".

IV

16. When will it be realized that Sri Ram and Sri Krishna are national heroes who brought victory and also glory to our motherland 'Hindutwa' is not a religion, it is 'Indian-ness', as held with remarkable clarity in the landmark judgments in—

***Shastri Yagnapurushdasji* v. *Muldas*, 1966 (2) SCJ 502: (1966) 3 SCR 242: AIR 1966 SC 1119 (para 27 to 40).**

***Kultar Singh* v. *Mukhtar Singh*, AIR 1965 SC 141: 1965 (1) SCJ 565: (1964) 7 SCR 790.**

***Ramesh Yashwant Prabhoo Dr.* v. *Prabhakar Kashinath Kunte*, AIR 1996 SC 1113: 1996 AIR SCW 652: (1996) 1 SCC 130 (169, 384, 394, 399).**

These cases quote *Webster's Third New International Dictionary,* the Encyclopedia Britannica, Max-Mullar and other authorities and approved what was said by Mulla in *'Principles of Hindu Law'*. The same thinking laid by Dr Keshav Hedgavar (the founder of the 'Rashtriya Swayam Sewak Sangh', "Hindutva is Rashtriyatva (Nationalism)", this is the true nature of Hinduism; the state has always been secular in Hindu polity. (*See* chapter VI Taming of a Tiger, in the authors book *'Ivory Tower 51 Years of the Supreme Court of India'* pages 44 to 51)

17. The Hindu festivals are not religious congregations. They are national festivals inspite of the religious tinge ascribed to them. The religious tinge was part of the 'hate everything Hindu' campaign of the invaders as a part of their conquest. In the year 1925, Lala Hardayal (the famous revolutionary) published an article in the 'Modern Review' under the caption 'The Social Conquest of the Hindu Race'. It emphasized that the conquest of India was merely political and never complete. Even the Hindu converts never adopted the Muslim customs and ways and always looked down upon them

V

18. My grandfather's younger brother (Ch. Dhanraj Singh) (I called him Babaji) was devoted to archeology as a hobby. He was a position-holder in his graduate examination and was directly appointed headmaster of Balwant Rajput High School, Agra (then probably a Junior High School and now a degree college). After a year, he received a call from the English Vice-Chancellor of his University. (He was his favourite student). The Vice-Chancellor gave him the glad news that he had been appointed in the Provincial Civil Service as a probationer Tahsildar and asked him to sign his acceptance. His protest that he would consult his family members was in vain; he was told that it was a great honour. On police verification it was discovered that the British Government had recorded about our family that nobody from it was to be appointed in the Government service as a 'reward' for our forefathers having taken part in the First War of Independence of 1857. The Governor however wrote thereon that he had taken the consent and appointment could not be annulled, but he should be given an independent charge of a District after he had been tested. The result was that wherever he was posted, he visited the archaeological sites and learnt the local folklore. He had old atlas of the world and had collected the legends and local folklore of ancient civilizations including our own Sanskrit literature.

19. Once he asked me to read a passage from the translation of Sri Bhagwat Puran (published from Poona). It related to *'Varah Avatar'* (the first incarnation of God 'Vishnu') and asked me what it depicted. I told him, it was a fairy story. But he said, 'Is it not a description of volcanic action, by which the Himalayas and the Indo-Gangetic plain, according to the modern scientific theory, came into existence'. He told me, "this incarnation of Vishnu was a poetic nomenclature under which God gave us the Himalaya and the plain for humanity to live". When asked about the next incarnation, he smilingly told me, "The humanity is figuratively the ocean. Its churning first produced 'hostility' (विष poison), but further churning (understanding) gave the nectar (अमृत), the knowledge different people possessed. The metaphor continues (he said) this became possible by the next incarnation '*Kurm*', (turtle) lord of the oceans'. He gave us a rational interpretation of the theory of incarnations, who were great benefactors of humanity. In the end of series Sri Ram and Sri Krishna and Gautam Buddha are the historical figures who rendered Godly service to humanity; they symbolize the triumph of good over evil.

20. Babaji showed me old atlas that there was a river 'Yemen' (Yamuna said he) in north-east Arabia (also called 'Yemen'), on the banks of which lay the ancient city of Muttra ('Mathura'?) and pointed out the old folklore and legends of that country. He informed me about old 'Champa' modern 'Vietnam' and how in ancient times Hindus (and later Buddhists) went to Brahma-desh (Burma now Myanmar) and Siam (now Thailand), Malaya which contained Sinhpur (Singapore) the gateway to India, and the East Indie's. He told me the story of 'Angkor-Vat the Hindu Temple and 'Bali' Island and how civilization was brought to them. He further told me (from folklore) how Hindus sailed from Champa (Vietnam) to Peru in South America and Maya country (Mexico). The Mayan calendar bears an imprint of the Hindu calendar. He pointed out how when the Portuguese killed the king of Peru by entrapping him by fraud, the Queen surprised them by insisting on sitting at the funeral pyre (as '*Sati*') and had to be forcibly removed.

21. Babaji told me to look for the remaining vestiges of Indian culture and civilization the world over. He advocated a global look and to discover the historical content in the folklore and legends over of the ancient civilizations. I have described some of these in my Hindi book, "*Kalchakra, Sabhyat Ki Kahani*" published by Prabhat Prakashan, Ajmere Gate, Delhi

22. Where has this global attitude gone? Our education is based on what foreigners and invaders have said making us the proverbial 'frog in the well' instead of a scientifically rational and national outlook of our world-wide culture, which gave real civilization throughout the world. Some of the foreign historians have hailed 'The wonder that was India'.

VI

23. In the year 1950, a series of children's schools called "Saraswati Shishu Mandir" were started; thereby hangs a tale. Professor Rajendra Singh was a reputed professor of Physics in the Allahabad University and his taught occupied important positions in the Government. Once when he was at Delhi his student, a Secretary in the Union Government invited him for tea in the evening. The Secretary unfortunately was late for a few minutes. The Professor began chatting with his daughter, a primary school student in a mission school. He asked her about the pictures in the calendar hung there. She replied, "This is Mahatma Gandhi father of the nation, this is Pandit Nehru, our Prime Minster". When asked about the calendar with the picture of *'Ganga-Avataran'* and *Shivji,* she said, "He is Daddie's God." On being asked where her God was, she said, "It is hanging there in the class-room (obviously referring to emblem of Christ on the cross).

24. This led to primary and secondary schools for children imparting a true national education. Under the names of 'Saraswati Shishu Mandir' and 'Saraswati Vidya Mandir. The first Shishu Mandir was opened at Gorakhpur. Professor Rajendra Singh also donated his land in the name of his mother in Civil Lines, Allahabad, for that purpose.

25. One day I was surprised to find a Muslim friend of mine with his son with a request to get his son admitted in the neighbouring 'Saraswati Shishu Mandir', I told him there was a prayer to Saraswati which he would have to repeat before the school classes began. He said, "What is wrong with an ode to 'Vidya' (knowledge)". He told me that all his friends and relations wanted his son to be sent to *'maktab'* or *'madarsa'* (religious schools), where he would have to commit to memory the holy 'Koran' in a foreign language, not prevalent in the country and be a victim of religious dogma "Let him grow up a normal human being, learn sciences and humanities like other children and love the country. I do not want him to go to be a fundamentalist or worse a terrorist in an atmosphere of 'hate everything Hindu'.

VII

26. When the Constitution came into force, we took steps to integrate the country as a national entity through, *inter alia*, education. For that purpose the Government got published books in Hindi, the language of the Union, in all disciplines of knowledge. Some of the Universities introduced courses where the medium of instruction was Hindi. I have standard Urdu-Hindi and English-Hindi dictionaries of law. My father (a master of Urdu and Persian) had already begun using Hindi words; he filed all plaints, applications, written statements, affidavits *i.e.* all legal documents in Devnagari Script when he took up legal practice at Banda. I followed that habit. After coming into force of the Constitution some law reports were published under the authority of the Union Government in Hindi.

27. But gradually everything was lost. A statute called Official Language Act was introduced in the Parliament permitting the continuance of English as an alternate language in the Union. That banished Hindi in its own land. 'Hindsthani' which was discarded and not recognized as a language by the Constituent Assembly, was a brainchild of the then Congress, and had been introduced by the Government in the former province of Madras, was introduced and became one of the recognized language in the Schedule in the Constitution as Urdu in a foreign script. It must be remembered that Urdu was one of the factors, which created Pakistan and in turn divided it further by creation of Bangladesh.

28. All the good work done in the Fifties to make Hindi a living contact language of Bharat was lost. The universities, the courts and the State Governments, where Hindi was already the State language reverted back to English to remind us that we were at a time ruled by the British.

The provision in the Constitution and the law for Hindi translation of all government orders and statutes has been thrown into oblivion. Even Urdu became the State language of Jammu and Kashmir and was introduced as the second language in some Hindi states contrary to the Constitutional provision.

29. How could this happen that the national interest have been completely eroded from education?

30. In my High School course in 1932-34 three poetry books were prescribed (i) 'Ayodhya Kand' of Sri "Ram Charitra Manas" of Tulsidas in Awadhi dialect, (ii) "Bal Krishna", the earlier life of Sri Krishna by Surdas in Brij-Bhasha, and (iii) "Jayadrath Vadh" by Maithili Saran Gupta (called rashtra-kavi) in Khari Boli dialect. It signified that they were dialects of Hindi and oneness of the three main dialects spoken in Northern India. Besides in our textbooks was included a poem of 'Vidyapati', the Maithili poet. The Awadhi and the Brij Bhasha had their own literature. But think now of agitation going for recognizing Konkani dialect of Marathi, as a separate language although (I am told) it probably has no separate literature of its own.

31. Article 345 relating to Official Language of the State provides that it may by law adopt any one or more of the languages used in the State or **Hindi** language as the official language. This obviously means either adopt one or more language prevalent in the State or Hindi as the Official Languages (obviously a concession to former multilingual states). If Hindi is adopted as the official language there can be no other second official language. Instead of providing impetus to integration, second language in Hindi States is reversing Constitutional obligations and mandate.

32. And what has happened to the national solar calendar sought to be adopted in the fifties. How many centuries must have gone to make the fusion of the solar and the lunar calendar. It was the global vision of India that made it possible. The ancient Hindu year was reckoned from the date when day and night were equal for both the Northern and the Southern hemispheres of the globe ('Varsh-Pratipada').

It was their science, which gave them a world vision. Their New Year day comes near about March 23 depending upon the *'malmas'* (extra lunar month). This calendar is a wonder produced by centuries or ages, when use of telescope was unknown.

33. Parts of this Hindu calendar were adopted the world over. The Muslim world adopted the lunar part only as ordained by their religion with the result that without the correction of the extra month (*malmas*) their year consists of 360 days. Their days of festivals or celebrations fall in different seasons. The 'Maya' of Mexico adopted the Hindu calendar.

34. Our 'Makar Sankraniti' is the day when the sun moves northwords (*'Uttarayan'*) from the *'Makar Rekha'* (Tropic of Capricorn). This Hindu festival was celebrated throughout in all ancient civilization of the world. They lay incidentally in the Northern Hemisphere. When the Church became powerful in Europe, they hijacked this Hindu festival and made it their own, assuming that Jesus Christ was born on that day. Recent researches show that constellations on the birth of Jesus Christ existed in the sky on 9th September 3 B.C., which is actually the day of his birth.

35. Now if we count six days leaving aside the 25th of December, assumed date of birth we come to the first day of January when according to Hindu custom a new-born child is given a taste of honey (the day of *'chhathi'*). This became the Christian New Year day. According to Hindu custom six days thereafter comes the day of *'barhon'* (literally after twelve days), This is the Christians' festival of 'Epiphany'. The Church adopted these Hindu days as their festivals. Thus, the Christian New Year's day comes in the middle of winter for the Northern Hemisphere and in the middle of summer for the Southern Hemisphere. Incidentally when Sri O.H. Mootham J. assumed the charge of the Chief Justice of the Allahabad High Court, he deleted 1st January from the list of holidays (closed day). When the lawyers protested this deletion, the Chief Justice merely replied, "Is it your 'New Year Day?"

36. Should our children not be told of the wonder of the Hindu calendar and the world vision it had. Even if we want a purely solar calendar, we ought to have adopted the national calendar of the Fifties (with day to day correspondence with the world calendar) beginning from 23rd March, the more rational and scientific vista for the whole world to adopt.

VIII

37. Take any day's newspaper and we find often the news of atrocities on women and children, of gang rape and child-abuse. One begins to wonder what has education made of our young men, beasts instead of cultured and educated men. We have changed education for the worse. The best cure of all such ills is to fire the young minds with a mission in life with patriotism and meaning to their existence. Instead of this our education of today morally degrades them.

38. On a *topsy-turvy* idea of secularism we have discarded our heroes and values of life and culture under false notions. At first, commissions or committees were formed of educationists. A need was felt to change the system of education. These were gradually replaced by Governments' orders and politicians to serve as a one-man commission. Education has been the first casualty at their hands.

39. We can hear the cries of people in an uproar getting shriller day by day about the gang-rape case committed in a Delhi Bus. One wonders how it could happen. What were the other passengers, if any, or people in the neighbourhood, and the conductor or the driver were doing?

40. I remember an incident in the early Sixties. I was travelling in a bus in Western Uttar Pradesh, probably from Chandausi to Bareilly. When the bus stopped at a small town, the conductor asked the passengers of that town to get down in the middle of the bazaar, as he said the bus would not stop at its station, which lay on the other side. The enquiries revealed an incident a few days ago. The bus had stopped at its station beyond the town, when a hoodlum entered the bus flourishing a pistol. He caught hold of a young woman laden with ornaments and forced her down the bus and dragged her towards the nearby sugarcane fields. Then some passenger cried. A young man chanced by and asked, 'what happened?' The passenger narrated the incident. The young man angrily remarked, "You twenty or so passengers looked on?" The passengers said, "The *badmas* (scoundrel) and pistol were two while each of them was alone".

41. Just then a shepherd came by. The young man asked him to give his stick (लाठी) and the scarf and donning it ran towards the field. On sighting the hoodlum, he cried, "Khan Sahib, have you seen my she-buffalo?" The hoodlum pointed his pistol firmly holding the young woman and asked him to go his way. Then suddenly the young man pointed the other side. "There is my she-buffalo". As soon as the hoodlum turned his head in that direction, the young man gave a lathi-blow on his head. He fell down. The young man just cried, "Sister, run. (snatching her), I am coming behind". At the bus he merely told the passengers, "Here is your young woman and the *'badmas'* (scoundrel) lies with his pistol in the field. He hurriedly took his shirt from the shepherd and went his own way. When the young woman regained her composure, she began weeping, "Where is my brother gone, who saved my life".

42. What is this education, which makes us cowards? The education does not teach us culture or mould our character. The Union Government introduced a course of what was called 'sex-education' in the secondary schools. A bizarre incident was reported in the newspapers. In a town of Madhya Pradesh, a brother just lifted the frock of his younger sister. On remonstration he said, he wanted to see if what was told in the class about different in sex was true. The teaching of sex-education in the schools was thereafter banned in Madhya Pradesh.

43. Our righteous indignation is not roused at the atrocity perpetrated on fellow countrymen. The empowerment of women cannot be achieved by conferring property rights on her. In my childhood in Bundelkhand a woman laden with ornaments could walk the streets alone at night and nobody could touch her. The Bundelkhand had forests. Every woman knew how to wield a stick *(lathi)* to ward off wild animals or potential danger. Our elders used to say, they have been independent for a century and a gift of independence is fearlessness. (अभय). After all the Ramayan (Lanka-Kand) and the Mahabharat occurred to vindicate the honour of women. What is this independence, which does not endow fearlessness?

44. There is a Sanskrit word *'Sanskar'* (literally) to make equal or produce equality), which has no parallel in English or any language known to me. The whole aim of education is to impart *'sanskar'* of a collective life and values and the qualities of a cultured human being. It cannot be achieved without citing the examples of our heroes. Yet in the name of parity of religions, we have discarded our true history and patriotism.

45. Swami Vivekanand was asked of the difference between Indian and western culture at the world conference in USA. He, *inter alia,* told the world religious community that in India every woman (except the wife) is either a mother or a sister or daughter. But what about the Christian (Biblical) lore in the West that God created Eve (woman) for enjoyment or entertainment of Adam.

46. Under the early Christian law a woman was not supposed to have a soul, she was not a person but property. It was this, which gave rise to Women's Liberation Movement (or in short the Women's Lib).

IX

47. The *'Shiksha Bachao Andolan'* (a Non-Governmental Organization, NGO) of Delhi had to carry a relentless agitation against the *flim-flam* introduced by the Union in the textbooks under excuse of easing out there school bag. They got filed a writ petition Nos. 17909-13 of 2005, ***Deena Nath Batra* v. *Union of India*** in the Delhi High Court. On a sharp criticism by the Judges the Union withdrew these books from curriculum. But I understand the Union has replaced them by Governmental orders. I also filed another proceeding (Writ Petition No. 25086 of 2006, ***Sanjiv Kumar Pandey* v.**

Union of India), still pending in the Allahabad High Court. The flagrant falsehoods and insults to the nation in these textbooks are too numerous. Some of them are catalogued in 104-page tract "The Return of the Reds" (communists are believed to be responsible for new textbooks under the Union Minister) and others published by them.

48. The Pioneer of Allahabad dated 28-11-2005 carried a news item on the first page under the banner headlines '*Jholawallahs*' (ignorant men posing as experts) Junk Our Past, Add Reams Without Rhyme'. It related to the Central School curriculum relating to 'Social Science Pedagogy'. It *inter-alia* read.

49. "Class VII students have a chapter called 'The Creation of an Empire' where everything about all the Mughal kings, their relations with other rulers, administration and the court, agrarian relations and a 'case study of Akbar' is mentioned. It is followed by a chapter on architecture and another 'case study' this time on 'Shah Jehan'. The greatest injustice is meted out to the Sikhs. Under 'popular beliefs and religious debates', a chapter for class VII, there is no mention of Guru Nanak at all, though Kabir is a 'case study'. The Khalsa Panth did not happen, Guru Govind Singh and Guru Tej Bahadur, who were insulted repeatedly by Marxist Satish Chandra, have been simply ignored this time. As for the great Banda Bahadur, he too did not exist. The valiant Jats are given short shrift as well.

50. "So, despite the homogenous sweep of the syllabus, the panel of historians recruited by HRD Minister Arjun Singh has taken care to whitewash any trace of the genie of nationalism. This follows from the *Jholawallah*-Marxist theory that before the British rule, the Indian people did not have a conception of nationhood. The textbook writers—whoever they are is a top secret even to NCERT's own Social Science department have been given the latitude to depict the Tughlaqs and Mughals as 'Indians' and whoever resisted their pillage as inconsequential. Is it possible to read Indian history without Mahmud of Ghazni's plunders? NCERT seems to think so. Prithiviraj Chauhan is irrelevant. Even Kautilya, the author of the *Arthashastra*, one of the world's most famous works on politics and statecraft, is obliterated from the study on ancient India. Adi Shankaracharya, who united India by setting-up the four *Maths* and preaching *Advaita* is found undeserving of mention. Moving to the modern era, one finds the *Brahmo Samaj* and its founder, Raja Rammohan Roy, given the quiet ignore. Doubtless, Roy's name would be packed in during a discussion on 'debates around *sati*' (Chapter 7 for class VIII) but what about his profound views on the *Upanishads*? The list of historic personalities, their contributions and events left out and the caricature is long enough to be a national shame. It is as if the collective memory of India has undergone a silent implosion.

51. "No government anywhere has done so much to massacre its own past".

52. The news item is an under statement. These textbooks are part of the 'social conquest of Bharat', that, which the foreign Muslim and Christian rulers (it seems) sought to achieve. For a political leader having been elected once is a know-all. His pride is sky high. The Union Government has replaced the educationist by politicians. Communism is also a religion. It has a prophet, Karl Marx, a book *'Das Capital'* as sacrament and the party leaders as sole interpreters of that 'religion'. The insults heaped by this education on everything in the past, the culture, and our forefathers by ridicule or omission will make the blood of every patriot boil.

53. The remnants and last vestiges of the foreign rule are strewn all over India. We have not been able to shake them. Sri Yogesh Saxena, Advocate, who spent his earlier age at Agra and had occasion to go inside the basement of Taj Mahal from the Yamuna side, filed 'Public Interest Litigation' in the Allahabad High Court. (Writ Petition No. 36814 of 2004, ***Institute of Rewriting World History, Goodwill Society Aundh, Poone through PN Oak President* v. *Union of India,*** decided on 21-02-2005). It prayed that certain statutes relating to Archeological Survey and Historical monuments in the name of Muslim invaders without scientific and historical investigation be declared *ultra vires*. For example, it was alleged that Taj Mahal was Tejo Mahalaya (Maan Mandir built for Man Singh from whom it was purchased) and Kutub Minar is the 'Vijay Stambha' of the Hindus. The list of Hindu Architectural monuments forcibly converted in the names of the invaders is very long. I have myself seen the Hindu symbols and architectural designs lurking from the portion where the outer plaster had peeled off in the alleged structure at Ram Janam Boomi, Ayodhya. Some historians claim that the Muslim invaders had no architecture of their own and did not build any monuments. They merely converted the buildings in their own name. History knows how invaders usurped the monuments. Should not an investigation be carried out to find the truth behind the allegations? The writ petition was however dismissed *in limine* with liberty to approach the appropriate forum.

54. Should our children not know the glorious achievements in science and humanities (Social Sciences) of our forefathers centuries before the Christian era? Should history not teach them that we gave the republican form of Government to the world? (*See* Hindu Polity by Dr. Kashi Prasad Jaiswal, a textbook prescribed for post-graduate classes in Universities during the British Rule).

55. Sri Lal Bahadur Shastri, the then Prime Minister of India had promised to attend the Vishwa Hindu Parishad meet at the Magh Mela grounds, Allahabad. In fact Sri M.S. Golwalkar (Sri Guruji, Sarsanghchalak of the Rashtriya Swayam Sewak Sangh) had advised him not to go to the foreign country. I know this because the letter was entrusted to me to be forwarded to him. It was understood that the Prime Minister would in commemoration of the event announce, naming the city as Prayagraj. But it was not to be, as he never came back from Tashkent. During his stint as Chief Minister, Sri Raj Nath Singh also promised to change the name. But the then Chief Secretary said, it could be done only by the Central Government. In fact 'land' is State subject and so are the Corporation and Municipalities. Mayawati during her Chief Ministership changed several names; which were upheld by the High Court

56. History bears out that 'Hinduism' is internationalism; it is 'humanism'. Think how people persecuted the world over took safe refuge in India. Thus the Syrian Christians hounded by Muslim hordes came to Kerala. That part was populated and ruled by Hindus. The refugees were given land and permitted to follow their faith. The Hindus built the Church for them. So was the 'Parsi' (Persians) who came and settled in the Western coast with their 'sacred fire'. Now they are at the top in India. And think of 'Karbala', where the persons besieged begged from their tormentors a safe passage to India. The Portuguese ambassador to what is called 'Vijaynagar empire' in the South is reported to have recorded, "If there is a heaven on Earth it is here in 'Vijaynagar', where even foreigners are treated as equal".

57. Wherever Hindus went, they gave the people culture, democracy and civilization, self-respect and qualities of head and heart. Why should our young men not know how much the world owes to India?

CHAPTER 8

Education and the Law the Supreme Court on Minority Institutions

I

1. This is also an examination of the eleven-Judge judgment of the Supreme Court in ***T.M.A. Pai Foundation* v. *State of Karnataka,* (2002) 8 SCC 481: 2002 AIR SCW 4957: AIR 2003 SC 355: and its sequel in *Islamic Academy of Education* v. *State of Karnataka,* AIR 2003 SC 3724: 2003 AIR SCW 4240: (2003) 6 SCC 697** regarding the rights of religious and linguistic minorities to establish and administer educational institutions of their choice, under article 30 of the Constitution of India.

2. It has to be read in the background of articles preceding it. Articles 25 to 28, grouped under the heading 'Right to Freedom of Religion' deal with the right to 'freedom of conscience and to profess, practice and propagate religion'. This right however is subject to public order, morality and health and 'to the other provisions of this Part', and does not affect the operation of any law and regulation restricting any economic, financial, political or any other secular activity associated with the religious practice. Further 'every religious denomination or any section thereof has a right to establish and maintain an institution for religious purposes and to manage its matters of religion'. The separation between the

State and religion is further emphasized by providing that 'no person can be required to pay taxes, the proceeds of which are specifically appropriated in payment of expenses for promotion or maintenance of any particular religion' and no religious instruction shall be provided in any educational institution run by the State.

3. Religion has been distinguished from culture and education, which are dealt within the two succeeding articles. Article 29 gives a right to all sections of citizens having a distinct language, script or culture of its own to conserve it. It further provides that any educational institution run by the State or receiving aid cannot discriminate in the matters of admission on the basis of religion, language and also race or caste. It will appear that the title of article 29 (*'Protection of interest of minorities'*) inserted later seems to be misfit, as the section does not talk of minorities but the right of all or any section of citizens to conserve their language or culture.

4. The rights of the minorities are spoken of in article 30. The word 'minority', wherever it occurs therein, is qualified by the phrase 'whether based on religion or language'. It thus appears that the minority spoken of, which has been granted rights under article 30 are only of two categories out of the various sections of citizens spoken of in article 29, namely 'minorities based on religion or language'.

5. The clear object of article 30 read with article 29 is to give religious and linguistic minorities a right to establish and administer educational institutions of their choice *for conserving their own religion or language.* These are part of culture of a community. This appears to be the reason why this right of religious and linguistic minorities has been grouped under cultural rights. There is no other reason for distinguishing their rights from the rights of others, spoken of in article 29, of conserving their language and culture. Moreover, in case of religious minorities this right is merely a corollary of the right conferred under clause (a) of article 26.

6. The protection guaranteed to a religious and linguistic minority is thus in respect of educational institutions imparting religious or linguistic instruction. It passes one's comprehension to find primary schools, high schools and colleges, teaching the ordinary course prescribed for public schools recognised under the statutes relating to primary, secondary or university education, treated as having some special rights, not possessed by other sections of the people. The said minorities are alleged to have special rights not enjoyed by others by the application of article 30 of the Constitution; and thus claim to be immune from State interference. If the object of protection granted under article 30 to a minority is to enable it to conserve its religion or language, it is in that connection that the religious or linguistic minorities can 'establish and administer their own educational institutions'. The State has no religion and in the matter of religious education, the State has ordinarily no say.

II

7. This is the doctrine of bifurcation and divorce between the State and religion. This is the true secularist principle. In America and Europe, there were Church schools under the management of religious institutions. In the Muslim countries, '*madarsas*' attached to mosques took their role. It is in order to disassociate public and scientific education from religious teaching that separation in education took place in the United States of America (USA). As a result, the public schools (that are run by or under the State management) disseminated education without religious beliefs. This followed from the first amendment of United States Constitution, "Congress shall make no law respecting an establishment of religion or prohibiting the free exercise thereof".

8. Article 30(2) prohibits discrimination between an educational institution run by a religious or linguistic minority and that run by others. These two categories of minorities differ in their composition and role. The religious minorities are sometimes at loggerheads with other religions and sometimes fight among themselves denouncing other's religious beliefs, dogma and other's God or Gods. The linguistic minorities are complementary to others and may be composed of opposing religious groups among them. With the re-carvation of linguistic States, and the directives regarding official language, public (or Government-run schools) and private schools can teach the curriculum in any tongue. Thus, the linguistic minorities can teach the same subject the public schools teach in their own language.

9. The same cannot be said of a religious minority giving instruction in their religion or through religious ministers. Religious education is often anti-thesis of secular education. Language is a vehicle of thought, religion is thought itself; nay, it may consist of dogma and a set of ceremonial or other practices (*'karmkand'*) attached to it. Moreover, priests, mullahs, imams, padri, or religious ministers usually administer institutions run by a religious minority. Their outlook is mostly coloured by stained glasses of religious dogma, bigotry and proselyting background. These religious minority institutions shorn of State control can only impart education with a slant.

III

10. We may examine how the *divorce* between public and religious education has worked in USA and how the opening part of their first amendment (*supra*) unfolded itself.

11. The story of assimilation of different sets of USA as a nation is told by William O. Douglas in his Tagore Law Lectures, *'From Marshall to Mukherjea: Studies in American and Indian Constitutional Law'*. He says:—

> "The story of the American melting pot is the story of how peoples of many tongues and many races became one. In America, the new arrivals often lived apart, clinging to their old customs and forming clannish groups in the community. Their work and future were in the United States; but their memories were still abroad:
>
> "But the second generation was different. The youngsters were part of the new community that was forming in America. *They attended the public school and learned one history, one language, one loyalty. The public school was the true melting pot; and the public school teacher was the leading architect*

> *of the new America that was being fashioned*. The races no longer stood apart. They were equals in the classroom. Merit rather than race also set the standard on the athletic field. The laurels went to the best student, whatever his or her race. Race became less and less important, as students were judged on their performance. The notion of *equality was more than a declaration of principle; it was a working creed*." (Emphasis supplied).

12. The original Constitution of United States of America (the USA Constitution in short) did not contain express guarantee of freedom to practice and propagate one's religion, although this was one of the motives that led to the founding of American Colonies. The first amendment repaired that omission in relation to the Congress, but left the States to their own constitutions. The Supreme Court of USA, however, held the free speech guaranteed by the Fourteenth Amendment applied the clause relating to free exercise of religion of the First amendment to the States also.

13. The freedom to pursue religion (his relation with God) and religious tolerance and, not only it, but also respect for all religions is the core of Indian-ness. Not so in Europe where religious sects had been persecuted. They came to America 'to escape the bondage of laws compelling them to support and attend government favoured churches'. They had carried memories of religious persecution, inquisition and punishment in matters of conscience and thought to the New World. Ultimately came Madison's 'Memorial and Remonstrance' against the renewal of Virginia's tax levy for support of established church and led to that State's Bill for Religious Liberty (originally written by Jefferson). There is the history of two centuries of 'turmoil, civil strife and persecutions' by established sects to maintain their 'absolute political and religious supremacy in America'.

14. Thus, free exercise of religion became the cardinal principle of USA Constitution. Then came a long tradition of exercise of religious freedom, which has been jealously guarded by the Supreme Court of USA. The courts, however, developed what is known as the 'Secular Regulation Rule'. This rule springs from the distinction drawn between belief and action. While religious beliefs enjoy absolute freedom, actions of religious denominations must conform to general regulations established by the community for its protection relating to secular matters. [*See* article 25(2)]. This rule ran into vacillating judgments, but the fundamental theme remained.

15. Jefferson is attributed to have said, "The legislative powers of the government reach actions only, not opinions; (and the citizen) has no natural right in opposition to his social duties". There are religious beliefs that run amok with life, and are used to justify sometimes bizarre and even cruel and dangerous practices. Some ideas going by the name of religion are unscientific and may even verge on insanity. Thus legislation, which is alleged to impinge secular regulation, could be challenged, if it had no nexus with the valid public purpose or if it resulted in discrimination between different religions or sects on its face. While acknowledging that total separation was not possible, the Supreme Court of USA, nevertheless, tried to build a 'high wall' between the government and religion, and to prevent, as far as possible intrusion of either the State or religious institutions into the precincts of the other.

16. In the field of education, the States drew a public programme, which might have been objectionable to certain religiously minded people. But, in case the State was to exempt certain groups on account of their religion, it could be viewed as giving assistance to it. This contravened the establishment clause of the first amendment. The neutrality of the State between religions could not debar public regulations.

17. In ***Lemon* v. *Kurtzman*, 29 Law Ed 2d 745** the Supreme Court of USA had occasion to deal with "State statutes providing State aid to church-related elementary and secondary schools with regard to instruction in secular (public) matters". It said:

> "In the absence of precisely stated constitutional prohibitions, we must draw lines with reference

to the three main evils against which the Establishment Clause was intended to afford protection, "sponsorship, financial support, and active involvement of the sovereign in religious activity. ... Three such tests may be gleaned from our cases (as criteria). *First*, the statute must have a secular legislative purpose; *second*, its principal or primary effect must be one that neither advances nor inhibits religion, and *finally*, the statute must not foster 'an excessive government entanglement with religion'."

18. The court further said,

"(It) cannot refuse to recognize that teachers (in church-related elementary schools) have substantially different ideological characters from books and cannot ignore the danger that a teacher under the religious control and discipline poses to the separation of religion from purely secular aspects of pre-college education. ... The Court will recognize that a dedicated religious person teaching in school affiliated with his or her faith and operate to inculcate its tenets will inevitably experience great difficulty in remaining religiously neutral.

"The merits and benefits of church-related elementary and secondary schools in national life are not an issue in determining the constitutionality of statutes providing for financial aids to such schools with regard to secular instructions."

It held that:

"The State aid to such schools cannot be squared with the dictates of the religious clauses of the first amendment."

19. The evidence produced in the case showed that:

"The church schools involved in the programme are located close to parish churches. This understandably permits convenient access for religious exercises since instructions, faith and moral are part of the total educational process. The school buildings contain identifying religious symbols; such as crosses on the exterior and crucifies and religious paintings and statues either in the classroom or hallways. Although only approximately 30 minutes a day are devoted to direct religious instruction, there are religiously oriented extra-curricular activities. Approximately two-thirds of the teachers in these schools are nuns of various religious orders. Their dedicated efforts provide an atmosphere in which religious instructions and religious vocations are natural and proper part of life in such schools.

"(The District Court) concluded that the parochial schools constituted 'an integral part of the religious mission of the Catholic Church'. The various characteristics of schools make them 'a powerful vehicle for transmitting the Catholic faith to the next generation'. This process of inculcating religious doctrine is of course enhanced by the impressionable age of the pupils in primary schools particularly. In short, parochial schools involve substantial religious activity and purpose."

20. How tenacious is religious dogma is illustrated by what is known as the 'Monkey Trial' in the judicial history of USA. It is called the monkey trial because of frequent question asked in the Christian world on publication of 'Origin of Species' by Charles Darwin, "Are we descendants of apes?" but more of it later. It comes a lesson which India cannot afford to forget.

IV

21. The correct interpretation of article 30 of the Constitution has long been bogged in acrimonious debates. There have been a series of the decisions of the Supreme Court relating to so-called "minority rights" to establish and manage their educational institutions. The difficulties seem to be cropping up in every turn and appear to be unending. Ultimately after a marathon hearing came the present decision of a Bench of eleven Judges; ***T.M.A. Pai Foundation* v. *State of Karnataka*, (2002) 8 SCC 481: AIR 2003 SC 355: 2002 AIR SCW 4957.** All the questions referred were, however, not answered; some of them were left over for the bench, which later heard the petitions.

22. That the argument has been simmering for years can be gauged by the fact that some of the matters in the bunch of cases coming up for decision had been pending since early eighties and one from 1979. During the hearing the Bench is reported to have recorded an order as follows:

> "Since a doubt has arisen during the course of our arguments as to whether this Bench would feel itself bound by the ratio propounded in, ***Kerala Education Bill, 1957,*** In *Re;* and ***Ahmedabad St. Xavier's College* v. *State of Gujarat,*** it is clarified that this sized Bench would not feel itself inhibited by the views expressed in those cases since the present endeavour is to discern the true scope and interpretation of article 30(1) of the Constitution, which being the dominant question would require examination in its pristine purity. *The factum* is recorded." What a reason – is it the law?

23. However the ultimate decision came by a five-Judge Bench in ***Islamic Academy of Education* v. *State of Karnataka*, (2003) 6 SCC 697: AIR 2003 SC 3724: 2003 AIR SCW 4240.** The two judgments did not strike a new line, nor examined the matter from first principles. The whole object of reference to a large Bench appears frustrated. The questions had to be examined afresh from the base. The ordinary approach of law courts runs into grooves, because of application of precedents. There is an old saying in logic and so in law, 'If we ask wrong questions, we are likely to land into wrong answers'. Wrong questions derail the argument. It appears that the initial and basic question never came to be adverted to or answered.

24. The first consideration is the concept of a 'right'. If there is a right guaranteed to a 'minority' by the Constitution, it must be a right; so equally of the 'majority' or of any section thereof. Equality is the largest integrating force with all diversities of life in a nation. The Advocate-General of Gujarat in case of ***Ahmedabad St. Xavier's College Society* v. *State of Gujarat*, (1974) 1 SCC 717: AIR 1974 SC 1389: (1975) 1 SCR 173** rightly argued that in case, a certain right to a minority is conceded, the majority would necessarily have that right.

25. The court in ***Pai Foundation*** case had tried to whittle down the rigid posture in ***Ahmedabad St. Xavier's College*** case. It held that regulations framed in national interest applied to all educational institutions whether run by the majority or a minority.

"Such a limitation must necessarily be read into article 30. The right under article 30(1) cannot be such as to override national interest or to prevent the Government from framing regulations in that behalf."

Paradoxically, it says,

> "It is, of course, true that the Government Regulations cannot destroy the minority character of the institution or make the right to establish and administer a mere illusion; but the right under article 30 is not absolute as per the above law."

This is further reiterated that:

> "Even though the words of article 30(1) are unqualified at least certain other laws of the land pertaining to health, morality and standard of education apply...By same analogy, there is no reason why regulations or conditions concerning generally the welfare of the students and teachers should not be made applicable in order to provide a proper academic atmosphere; as such provisions do not any way interfere with the right of administration or management under article 30(1)."

26. Beautiful words, but they leave the problem where it lay unanswered. 'What is the practical solution?' The highest national interest is served by 'equality before the law'. The dictum of the court is nebulous and, to say the least, beset with uncertainties and fluidity. Certainly, proper academic atmosphere is desirable in national interest. But how to ensure it in a minority institution run by a religious denomination with churches or places of religious worship attached, manned by padries, *mullas* and priests or religious missions. It seems that the whole exercise in the case almost ended in futility and except for some points, the thinking ran the same course as before. There came no basic original thoughts, no departure from the rut to examine the reason of the provision. The Court did not take the courage into its hands to think of a pragmatic solution from the roots. It forgot that article 25 is the general provision while article 30(1) is a part of it.

V

27. The interpretation of these articles is undoubtedly beset with difficulties. But the words in a statute are not used in isolation. They are related to the subject of legislation and the object to be achieved. It was said in ***United States* v. *Shirey*, 3 L.Ed. 2d 289** that:

> "Statutes are not inert exercises in literary composition. They are instruments of Government, and in construing them 'the general purpose is a more important aid to the meaning than any rule, which grammar or formal logic may lay down'... This is so because the purpose of enactment is embedded in its words, even though it is not always pedantically expressed in words.... Statutory meaning, it is to be remembered is more to be felt than demonstrated or....'the art of interpretation is the art of proliferating a purpose'."

28. Our Supreme Court has said in a series of decisions that the words, phrases or sentences used in a statute should be considered in the light of its general purpose and a mechanical interpretation of the words devoid of concept or purpose will reduce most of legislation to futility. Accordingly, the Supreme Court went to the extent of saying that 'words and phrases even though comprehensive must be construed as being limited to the actual object of the statute.' This is the doctrine of purposive interpretation.

29. All exercise in interpretation of statutes is to discover the true intention of the Legislature. The flexibility of language requires for its interpretation aid of various *'Mimansa'* rules. In ***Carter* v. *Bradbeer*, (1975) 3 All ER 158 (HL)** Lord Diplock said:

> "If one looks back to the actual decisions on questions of statutory construction over the past thirty years, one cannot fail to be struck by the evidence of a trend away from purely literal towards the purposive construction of statutory provisions."

VI

30. The two articles 29 and 30 must be read in conjunction with each other, grouped as they are under one heading 'Cultural and Educational Rights'. Further they occur in the background of preceding articles relating to 'Right to Freedom of Religion'. Since every section of society has a right to conserve its culture (and religion is a part of culture), the religious minorities have been conferred the right to establish and administer educational institutions for that purpose.

31. The words 'of their choice' must have some connection with the type of minority spoken of. It is a pointer that educational institutions of a religious minority must relate to its religion. It does not give them a right to open schools imparting public education on terms different from others. The right of a religious minority 'to establish and administer educational institution of their choice' must relate to the object or purpose for which the provision exists, namely the right to preserve one's own religion. These words cannot confer on a religious group a right to roam in the territory of education and claim to be singled out in the realm of public education 'because of its religion'. In fact, public or scientific education has no religion.

32. It will be anomalous to think of a linguistic minority (whom the Constitution bestows the fundamental right to conserve the language) to establish and administer by virtue of article 30 'an educational institution of its choice' giving instruction in a foreign tongue or another language not their own. In the same way, it is anomalous to think of a religious minority establishing and administering educational institutions teaching courses prescribed for ordinary government or public schools, which have nothing to do with their religion and by virtue of article 30(1) claim special privileges and immunity from State interference. Harmonious construction demands that equality is preserved in this respect, and special privilege granted only in respect of their religious education, or training.

33. The ***Pai Foundation*** case (*supra*) as well as all the previous decisions proceed from the point of view of the 'rights' of a minority, and thus landed on a literal interpretation, contrary to the basic postulate of equality. The correct approach (it is suggested with respect) was the purposive interpretation. Once it is adopted, the whole gamut of articles (25 to 30) falls into a rational pattern. It becomes apparent that the right of a religious minority 'to establish and administer educational institutions of their choice' extends only to the purpose for which it was granted, namely to conserve their religion [article 29(1)] or for maintenance of religious institutions and efficient management and training in discharge of its own affairs in matters of religion [article 26, clauses (a) and (b)]. The true secularist mandate is also that religion cannot be allowed to dabble in the State affairs including education, and *vice versa*.

34. Political division along religious lines or the evil of involvement or entanglement between government and religion must be avoided. We have not learnt the lesson from judicial history of USA. The Supreme Court of USA has emphasised the dangers resulting therefrom. Once purposive construction is adopted, all the questions framed from time to time in ***T.M.A. Pai Foundation*** case are answered. No difficulties can arise and aberrations are wiped out. It is a single answer to the complex problems.

CHAPTER 9

Education and the Law: The Monkey Trial

I

1. What has the case known as the 'Monkey Trial' in the judicial history of United States of America got to do with us? Yet that trial and the decisions relating to teaching of the Darwin's biological theory of evolution and his book 'Origin of Species' carry a message, which the nation and our judiciary can ill-afford to forget. 'The Monkey Trial' is so-called because of frequent question asked in the Christian world on publication of 'Origin of Species' by Charles Darwin, 'Are we descendants of apes?'

2. [*The following description is borrowed from Yatindra Singh's book 'Lawyer's World and Childhood Dreams'*], A biology teacher (Scopes) taught in his school 'the theory of evolution' as propounded by Charles Darwin. The Tennessee anti-blasphemy law banned, *inter-alia,* "the teaching of any doctrine contrary to creation of man as told in the Bible". He was arrested and tried in an improvised courtroom on the lawn of the courthouse, where 5000 spectators along with the newsmen watched it. It was a spectacular trial and presented the most amazing court scene in American history.

3. The prosecutor thundered, "The trial uncovers an attack on religion. If evolution wins, Christianity goes". Clarence Darrow one of the most famous criminal trial lawyer retorted, "Scopes is not on trial; civilization is on trial". Scopes was convicted, but the decision was reversed in appeal on a technical ground. The Supreme Court of Tennessee, however, held by 3-1 that the anti-evolution law was not unconstitutional.

4. Such laws, which banned the teaching of the theory of evolution, as it was contrary to the chapter of 'Genesis' in the Bible, were repealed in 1976.

5. However the question erupted again in another form. The State of Louisiana had passed a law requiring the State public schools to give 'balanced treatment' to 'creation science' and 'evolution science'. The statute provided that if either of the two was taught in the school, the other must also be taught. The purpose of the statute was said to be protection of 'academic freedom'. The court in—

***Edwards* v. *Aguillard*, 96 L Ed. 2nd 510** came to be conclusion that provision of the statute that public schools were not required to teach either the 'theory of evolution' or 'creation science', but in case either was taught, the other also must be taught was in violation of the first amendment. It was establishing a religious doctrine.

6. The court held that the statute was 'primarily designed either to promote a particular religious tenet favoured by certain religious sects' or to prohibit the teaching of a scientific theory, hence it was unconstitutional. It held that the term 'creation science', contemplated by the legislature and adopted in the statute, embodied the religious belief that supernatural creator was responsible for the creation of human kind.

7. The opposition of fundamentalists against teaching the theory of evolution had gone on in one form or other ever since the book 'Origin of Species' was published till the year 1987, when the aforesaid case was decided by the Supreme Court of USA.

8. "In ascertaining this purpose it is important to remember that no matter how elastic is the use to which the term 'scientific' may be put, it cannot be used to describe the legislative process. This is a crude but practical process of adaptation by the ordinary citizens of means to an end..."

II

9. A Constitution is a living organism with the purpose of integrating a society in a continuous stream of life. It is all the more necessary that the provisions thereof should be interpreted dynamically in the light of the object of the provision with a view to advance its cherished goal and at the same time preserve basic national characteristics.

10. All exercise in interpretation of statutes is to discover the true intention of the Legislature.

In ***Tata Engineering and Locomotive Co. Ltd.* v. *State of Bihar*, (2000) 8 SCC 346**, the Supreme Court remarked:

> "Statutes, it is often said, should be construed not as theorems of Euclid but with some imagination of the purposes which lie behind them and to be too literal in the meaning of words is to see the skin and miss the soul. The method suggested for adoption, in cases of doubt as to the meaning of the words used is to explore the intention of the Legislature through the words, the context which gives the colour, the context, the subject-matter, the effects and consequences or the spirit and reason of the law. The general words and collocation or phrases, howsoever wide or comprehensive in their literal sense are interpreted from the context and scheme underlying in the text of the Act."

11. The subject of purposive interpretation or construction has been summarized in a decision of the Allahabad High Court in ***Suman Upadhyaya* v. *Vice-Chancellor, Purvanchal University*, (2000) AWC 1216** (paragraphs 11-19).

12. These will be institutions imparting education and training for the aforesaid purposes in matters of religion and for its preservation. India is not a theocratic State; it does not pander to any religion.

In ***Aruna Roy* v. *Union of India*, (2002) 7 SCC 368: AIR 2002 SC 3176: 2002 AIR SCW 3670,** the Supreme Court defined 'religious instruction' used in article 28(1) of the Constitution:

> "(The expression religious instruction) conveys that teaching of customs, way of worship, practices or rituals cannot be allowed in educational institutions wholly maintained out of State funds".

In fact, the right of religious minority to establish and administer educational institutions of their choice is confined to institutions giving this religious instruction and training therein or in fulfilment of the rights under clauses (a) and (b) of article 26 and article 29(1) of the Constitution.

13. The Supreme Court could not strike a new line of original thinking probably because of the legacy of the earlier judgments. The past was too much with it. The result is that there are a host of so-called 'minority institutions' outside the control of the State dotted throughout the country administered by religious ministers, which may be hotbed of fundamentalist and proselytizing activities under one garb or the other. They often breed extra-territorial loyalties. Their atmosphere, the teaching, the environment, extra-curricular activities all smack of religious fervour and separatist tendencies. The goal of national integration is the first casualty therein.

14. Religion must be distinguished from culture as mandated by separate mention in the Constitution. Culture and cultural activities are necessary ingredient of education. They must be distinguished from religion, which can be said to be a part of present culture. The valiant effort in ***Aruna Roy's*** case *(supra)* to distinguish between religion and culture is commendable. But the line between cultures, which may consist partly of what I have called 'personal culture' (as distinguished from social culture, which includes one's religion also) must be more sharply drawn.

15. It must be understood (as said by the Supreme Court) that Hinduism is not a religion, it comprises various (religious) beliefs and it is a way of life, which is another name for culture. It is Indian-ness. Sanskrit is one of the languages mentioned in the Eighth Schedule. The Constitution enjoins the drawing of vocabulary primarily from Sanskrit (article 351). *'Veda'* and *'Purana'*, the *'Ramayan'* and *'Mahabharat'* the *'Gita'* and the *'Upnishads'* are all parts of culture and national inheritance of the country. They do not contain religious dogma or injunctions for some exclusive society, but are heritage of mankind. Yet, paradoxically, Hindu-baiting equates them with religion. The efforts to imbibe the ancient science and culture are termed as 'saffronization'. It appears that a campaign has been drawn against 'nationalism'.

16. Looked from the background of religious rights under articles 25 and 26, and as said earlier the phrase that a religious minorities "shall have a right to establish and administer educational institutions of its choice" can only refer to the establishment of institutions imparting religious education. Every religious denomination is free to have its schools for training in or teaching their religion. The protection of article 30 cannot be said to extend to an educational institution imparting secular (or scientific) education. Article 30 in the context of religious minority appears not to deal with it.

17. The religious minority schools pose a threat to the secular character of the nation. It is all the more so at the primary or secondary stages where school children of an impressionable age are doctrinaired in the beliefs of a particular church. If religious beliefs are to be taught as a subject at all, let a comparative study be taught at the university stage where minds are mature and can follow or choose according to dictates of their conscience. At the primary or secondary stages the future generation of citizens must be taught their cultural heritage, shorn of blatant untruths of history and dogma. Culture and nationalism are the largest binding force of a nation.

18. We have not learnt the lesson judicial history of USA offered and have forgotten the part played by an ordinary teacher in the primary and secondary public schools (not schools run by religious institutions), which were true 'melting pot' in inculcating equality as a creed. Let us not forget the danger which scientific education under the guise of 'minority educational institutions', and by religious leaders without any check, poses to the nation. Let no handle be given to any religious group to pave the way for situations giving rise to 'jehad' or a 'monkey trial'. The hotchpotch in the field of education and the dangers and pitfalls could have been avoided by giving a purposive interpretation to article 30 to bring out harmony in the Constitutional provisions.

19. *'Fatwa'* means a religious edict in the Muslim world. It is also an order or decision pronounced by a Muslim religious minister in accordance with the canons of Islam. It encompasses the whole of Muslim world, not only regarding the religious rites, but the whole social and political outlook, the entire life (see 'The World of Fatwas' by Arun Shourie). In fact it can more or less function as a government by Muslim religious leaders for Muslims within the State. It functions as a Muslim country in a secular State. For a Muslim, there are two governments, a religious government within the State; nay a parallel government. How could this happen under the garb of religion?

20. Look to the world history, we can see that it is the first step towards creation of an Islamic government. It is formation of a religious State within the country. After all it is the basis of a two-nation theory of the Muslim League, which resulted in partition of the country.

21. The proselytizing religions tend to be rigid. Communism is also one such religion, which has one sacrament *'Das Capital'*, and the party is the sole interpreter of it. The latest advancement in science and sociology has no place there.

22. The Supreme Court of USA had to invent a 'Regulation Rule' in order to give effect to ordinary governance. We do not have to invent it, as it is embodied in article 25(2) of our Constitution. Article 30 cannot be disassociated from it, as has been done by our Supreme Court. This gave rise to the grave problem of certain religious minority institutions out of control of the legislature. These also constitute a grave danger to the country. Our courts have failed to realize that it is regulatory rule invented by Supreme Court of USA put by the Constituent Assembly in this form. Our Supreme Court has created some problems in the field of education and the majority judgment in ***Indra Sawhaney's*** case (*supra*) is the worse culprit.

23. When will our Supreme Court and the High Courts realize the grave danger lurking in the field of education of disintegration of the country?

CHAPTER 10

Lest We Forget

I

1. I did not want to pen down this chapter. But many friends insisted, "If you do not write about illustrious judges and failings of some of them, nobody else can. Your experience encompasses two ages, the age of the British Rule and thereafter coming into force of the Constitution of India. Nobody knows the phases of freedom struggle and the Constituent Assembly debates, which took place when you were already enrolled as a lawyer. How will the coming generation of the lawyers and judges know the background of our Constitution and what are the qualities required of them" I cannot arrogate to myself the role, but I in the end was persuaded to pen the following few lines.

II. The Max Muller School

2. Some of the earlier illustrious Judges, who come to join the Indian Judiciary at Allahabad from the Bar of the United Kingdom, were drawn to it in no less measure by the writings of Max Muller and others and the texts of ancient Hindu Law. They were nicknamed as belonging to the Max Muller School.

3. The most illustrious of them were Sir John Edge (Chief Justice) and his companion Judges. They will always be remembered for the fond hope they expressed that a day would come when the texts of the Hindu Law would be interpreted by *'Jamini's Mimansa'*, (one of the six schools of philosophy *'shad-darsan'*) and the rules of interpretation contained therein. They probably had Colebrook's translations of the texts. Their judgments on Mitaksshara Law, which prevailed in Northern India, are a model of elucidation. They made the Allahabad High Court famous. One such judgment on adoption is the Full Bench decision in,

***Beni Prasad* v. *Hardev Bibi,* ILR 14 All 67: 1892 AWN 161 (FB),** in which the Jamini's *'Mimansa'* was copiously quoted.

4. I remember I purchased the Colebrook's translation of *Jamini's Mimansa* and Hindu Law texts at the Parade Ground at Kanpur. In early Fifties I chanced to find that a *kabadi's* second hand shop had an old library of law books. He told me that they were for sale at Re 1 or Rs. 2 per book. When I began to select books from the collection, he said that the selection would cost me Rs. 5 each. I would have paid even Rs. 100 had he named that price for Colebrook's translations of ancient Hindu Law texts. Once I quoted these in the Supreme Court, the judges were electrified. They said, 'the Supreme Court did not have them' and asked me if I would donate them. I said I would gladly donate, if I could get them to quote whenever I attended that court. The Judges said they could not guarantee it and there the matter ended.

5. To come back to the Max Muller School, one of their famous Full Bench decision is on 'possessory title'. It firmly established the rule. I remember it for the invectives in the judgment by the Judges against one of them. (Syed Mahmood J) sitting on the same Bench. After the Second World War when Indian Independence Act was passed by Parliament of United Kingdom, a daily newspaper of Delhi, *'The Hindustan Times'* published a book called 'Invective and Abuse in Judicial Pronouncements' (or some such heading). It related to aspersions cast on each other in the acrimonious atmosphere of the war. This judgment could be one of them. It is the famous Full Bench (probably full court) decision in

***Wali Ahmad Khan* v. *Ajudhia Kandu,* ILR 13 All 537: (1891) 11 AWN 196 (FB).** It is a case which every lawyer should read.

6. Shri Gurdayal Srivastava, my neighbour, was all panegyrics for Justice Syed Mehmood. He had contributed an article on him in Commemoration Volume I of Post-Centenary Silver Jubilee Celebrations of the Allahabad High Court. He sent the draft of that article to me also. When I pointed out the aforesaid decision to him, he said that he did not know it. He thereafter left talking about Justice Mehmood.

III

7. Sir Grimwood Mears was appointed Chief Justice of the Allahabad High Court in 1919 just after the First World War. He remained its Chief Justice till 1932 (probably the longest term for a Chief Justice in India). It always happens that corruption sets in after a war, which disrupts the country. This happened after the First World War also. But Sir Grimwood Mears cleaned the whole judiciary, (Judges and advocates alike). At that time pleaders and advocates were both enrolled by the High Court. The Judiciary of this State, thanks to Chief Justice Sir Grimwood Mears, has been reputed to be the best and most honest judicial system in India.

8. One such incident concerns Banda, where I started my practice as a lawyer. A very prominent Vakil of Banda had filed a suit on a pronote in the name of his clerk against a litigant, a former accused in a criminal trial. The suit was filed in the Court of the Munsiff at Banda. The defense was that no money was paid under the pronote, but it was champerty transaction, the pronote being executed in lieu of the vakil's fees for conducting his case in the criminal trial. The defense that it was a champerty transaction was negatived and the Munsiff Sri Nandlal Singh decreed the suit. So rigid was the English Law against champerty that the Chief Justice debarred the lawyer from practice and transferred the Munsiff to another district. Sri Nandlal Singh was a learned officer. In his new posting he happened to decide a case citing original texts contrary to the observations of the High Court on Hindu Law. He had to pay for it and was not confirmed. The irony is that the Privy Council on appeal upheld the view of Sri Nandlal Singh, but he had already paid for his indiscretion.

The lawyer could be reinstated only after Sir Grimwood Mears had retired

9. Then we must remember the outstanding figures in the galaxy of lawyers of the High Court who brought glory to it. Two of them were Sir P.C. Banerjee and Sir Sunderlal Dave (who rose to be Judges of the High Court). Two Allahabad University hostels are named after their memory bear testimony to their munificence. And there was Sir Tej Bahadur Sapru whose role in the Round Table Conference and India's Independence cannot be forgotten.

IV

10. I joined the High Court Bar in 1950, almost when the Constitution became operative. I have recited in my 'Reminiscences of the Bar' entitled 'Flowers at the Altar' (of justice). In spite of great temptation to repeat about the illustrious Judges and lawyers I have talked about therein, I refrain from doing so as unnecessary. Some of their utterances have become classic and what they did for the judiciary will always be remembered with pride. I have been fortunate in having their love and affection. It is neither possible, nor called for to pay again my tributes to them here.

11. The period covered by the Reminiscences upto the middle of the first decade of twenty-first century is not without black spots, which disfigured it. I have alluded to some of them, which have been galling to my sense of justice. I have described my confrontation with one Judge in the chapter 'The Dark Interlude' and about some others elsewhere. But the references to these are without naming the Judges or Advocates. I have always regretted these episodes.

V

12. The legal profession is not a trade. It is a position of trust; trust not only to the litigant but also to the society. It is not open to any person belonging to the learned professions to behave like a trade unionist. The Supreme Court and the High Courts have deprecated lawyer's strike. *See* for example:

***Ex.-Captain Harish Uppal* v. *Union of India*, AIR 2003 SC 739 (CB).**

> "For just or unjust cause strike cannot be justified in the present day situation. Take strike in any field it can be easily realized that this weapon does more harm them any justice; sufferer is the society, public at large".

The Bar Associations and the Bar Counsel exists to ensure smooth running of the judicial process. Strike is a weapon of the under-privileged, who has no other remedy. The lawyer can use the Courts to redress their grievances. The call some times giving to them about strike is wholly unwarranted and illegal.

13. We are votaries of justice and any person holding a judicial office as arbiter sits in the seat of God. There is a famous Hindi story *'Panch-Parmeshwar'* by Munshi Prem Chand. Show of temper or tantrums do not behove a court scene, all lawyers and Judges should rise above it. When I got some success at the Bar, my father told me, "Son, if you achieve some position in life, you must imbibe equal greatness, dignity and magnanimity in life. To be vindictive is pettiness, shed it". The judiciary acts like a doctor or a medical practitioner or social life of a nation. The lawyers and Judges must rise to the occasion and fulfil the great task of building a just society and a great nation. Let them be fired with patriotic fervour to achieve it. Let us be equal to the task.

14. When a Judge of the highest court goes wrong, the only way to correct it is by criticism. Every person concerned with the judicial process should welcome it. Because it is this method by which the law advances in the society.

SUBJECT INDEX

•••